EX LIB

JAMIESON LIBRARY
Newmill · Penzance

NON-FICTION: A GUIDE
TO WRITING AND PUBLISHING

UNIFORM WITH THIS BOOK

Maps for Books and Theses by A. G. Hodgkiss
Photographs for Books and Reports by Brian
Bracegirdle BSc, FRPS

BY THE SAME AUTHOR

David St John Thomas is chairman and managing
director of David & Charles (Publishers) Ltd. His
own books include *A Regional History of the
Railways of Great Britain, Volume I: The West
Country* (first published 1960 by Phoenix House,
third edition 1966 by David & Charles), *The
Rural Transport Problem* (Routledge & Kegan Paul),
*Double Headed: Two Generations of Railway
Enthusiasm* (written jointly with Gilbert Thomas
and published by David & Charles), and—for
children—*The Motor Revolution* (Longmans),
Great Moments with Trains (Phoenix House) and
Trains Work Like This (Phoenix House)

DAVID ST JOHN THOMAS

Non-Fiction:
A Guide to Writing
and Publishing

DAVID & CHARLES : NEWTON ABBOT

7153 4802 7

*Set in eleven on thirteen point Intertype Times
and printed in Great Britain
by Clarke Doble & Brendon Limited Plymouth
for David & Charles (Publishers) Limited
South Devon House Newton Abbot Devon*

To my wife Pamela Mary
And also to my staff

Notes

Every care has been taken in the writing of this book
and many people have been consulted; but
accuracy cannot be guaranteed on taxation and
legal matters which are anyway subject to change.

Like all publishers, David & Charles are pleased to
receive manuscripts and suggestions for books
for consideration, but the author and the firm cannot
of course give a general advisory service on
points made in this work.

Contents

Examples of illustrations suitable for line and half-tone treatment are given opposite pages 76 and 77

Introduction

DEFINITIVE NON-FICTION

THE MAIN AIM of this work is to give practical advice to the growing number of people who write a book in their spare time on a subject connected with their profession, job or hobby. The kind of people I have in mind are teachers writing textbooks for use in classroom or school library, graduates turning their PhD theses into books, scientists bringing their colleagues up-to-date on technical developments, economists or sociologists with views on problems past or present, amateur historians ready to publish part of their researches, do-it-yourself experts with practical experience to pass on . . . the list is endless. Gardeners write on gardening, travellers produce guide books, cat breeders describe special points, railway historians lovingly portray branch lines as they were in their steam heyday, naturalists report on the behaviour of wild animals, doctors discuss diseases and their cure.

This objective, outward-looking kind of book is my main concern, partly because the current great expansion of literature is in this sphere, and partly because my own experience is with definitive non-fiction. But some aspects of writing and publishing are, of course, shared by books of all kinds, and possibly even new novelists or writers of children's stories may find that parts of this work are relevant. Established professional authors, too, may find one or two points useful or provocative, though I have assumed the reader to be new to authorship— to have something to communicate but not to be practised in the art of writing or in dealing with publishers.

There are of course many previous books on writing and publishing, but nearly all of them are either elementary textbooks or are concerned with fiction and 'literary' work. Here I hope I have adopted a middle-of-the-road approach that will be useful to many authors who will never figure in the best-seller lists but whose books will give pleasure to substantial minority audiences.

It is only fair to state that I write as a publisher who has dealt with many new authors. I have greatly enjoyed my association with most of them and have often gratefully realised that their spontaneity (because they are *not* full-time professional writers) more than compensates for any lack of polish. But any publisher has patiently to explain time and again simple facts about turning a manuscript into a book, because these facts are not adequately covered in any of the available reference works. Possibly, therefore, the book has been written partly to make my job and that of other similar publishers easier; certainly some of the views are purely personal ones, though where the advice departs from traditional publishing practice I have tried to make the reasons clear. But principally the aim is to help shape good ideas into good books.

I have also been stirred by that restless urge to communicate—the desire that will presumably have stirred most of my readers to become authors themselves.

AUTHOR, PUBLISHER, PRINTER AND BOOKSHOP

Most of this book assumes an elementary understanding of the roles of author, publisher, printer and bookshop. Yet publishing firms not infrequently receive orders to quote for printing manuscripts as though they were printers who merely accept the job submitted, rendering the bill at the end. So before starting, these are the basic facts for any who are in doubt—and the rest please skip.

An author is of course the writer of a book, but in the publishing world today he does not necessarily have that book published exactly as he first writes or conceives it. He writes to a publisher to discuss publication, and for a variety of reasons the publisher may ask for the book to be changed. The author may agree to undertake the revision himself; eventually, when the nature of the book has been mutually decided, the publisher's staff may do further revision. The author can decline to have any such interference with his work, or he may object to interference beyond a given point, and thus risk rejection of the book by that particular publisher. He should not, however, be surprised that the publisher dares to suggest making changes. The novelist, the poet or the author of 'pure' literature in any form would of course not normally expect his publisher to have much say in the actual detailed contents and presentation. Work of such kinds is too intimate a reflection of the author's personality. But here we are concerned with 'applied' literature; non-fiction works on specific subjects are only literary in that language should be used to the best advantage in presenting the facts. There need be no lack of artistic feeling, but the subject matter comes first and it is more important that the subject be covered clearly, thoroughly and in a rational order than that the work is written in any particular style or with any special literary effects. While, therefore, the author is the creator, he will frequently be expected to adapt his baby in accordance with the publisher's assessment of what is needed—and what will sell.

A publisher is an entrepreneur who normally publishes books that he has accepted or commissioned at his own cost and risk, usually paying the author a royalty on sales. He designs the books, chooses the paper and the binding materials, and determines the timetable of production and all other details, though frequently the author's view is taken into account on certain matters. The actual processes of printing and binding are sub-contracted to printers and binders, though to the detailed specifications of the publisher. A few publishers own printing works, but even then the publishing and printing sides of the business are under different management and the printing side acts as sub-contractor working to the requirements of the publisher. Publishers often buy their own raw materials such as paper and

have them consigned to printers. Once the books have been
printed and bound their consignment to the book trade is again
organised by the publisher. Some publishers have their own
warehouses and despatch depots; others sub-contract the storage
and despatch operations, never handling the bulk stock.

Bookshops buy almost exclusively from publishers on recognised terms and to a well-established pattern of trade, which for
certain classes of business also involves wholesalers. Occasionally bookshops undertake publishing on their own account,
and some publishers own bookshops as well as printing works;
but even where there is common ownership, the processes of
printing, publishing and bookselling are always segregated and
demand very different skills.

A WARNING

Any author in the accepted sense of the word arranges the
publication of his book with a publisher. Some people, however, fail to find a publisher willing to accept their work; and
a few then attempt to print and publish on their own account.
Quite apart from the fact that a book rejected by a cross-
section of commercial publishers is unlikely to pay its way,
this operation usually ends in disaster. The amateur finds it
difficult to give the right instructions to the printer, and too
often chooses the wrong kind of printer. He is likely to be even
vaguer over the trade and publicity aspects, failing for instance
to understand the role of the book jacket for publicity purposes, and not knowing how the book's advent should be announced through the trade press to the wide world. Even if
he does eventually produce a conventional book at the right
kind of price, he will not have a representative soliciting orders
for him at bookshops throughout the land (the reluctance of
most booksellers to order for stock unless a representative calls
on them has to be experienced to be believed), he will probably
not be taken seriously even by those shops he may have time to
call upon himself, and he will lack knowledge of export procedures.

Sometimes an author can successfully publish a pamphlet or booklet intended just for limited sale—such as a guidebook which would anyway appeal only to shops in his own home town which he can visit regularly, or a small work of interest to members of his profession or society which he can market by post, using the membership mailing list or advertising in the specialist magazine. With such small, paper-covered works the stakes and expectations are comfortably low, and failure to find the national public library demand is irrelevant.

But with rare and small-scale exceptions, the author-publisher of a bound book will be dismissed as a crank; he will waste his money and other people's time. Any publisher hears pathetic tales of authors printing books and then trying to find a publisher to 'publish' them; of elderly men putting their last savings into producing their life history and having to give up their front room to storing the unwanted stock; of authors who have paid publishers to produce works on their behalf with practically no sales resulting. There are of course circumstances in which it is recognised as sensible and reputable for authors to help finance their own specialist works; but there are also a few publishers with whom it is best not to make such arrangements. This aspect is dealt with in chapter 8.

DO YOU HAVE A BOOK IN YOU?

But it would be wrong to end the introduction on a negative note. Ever more people from every conceivable walk of life are becoming successful authors, not because they have any special literary genius but because there is something they want to communicate or explain, and they have the determination and commonsense to bring a book to fruition. Many are rightly proud of their books. Some have won promotion in their jobs or professions as the result of publication, and others have acquired a high standing among followers of their hobby. Bank balances are also usually the happier for authorship, especially if the most has been made of opportunities to save tax.

Do you have a book in you? What tests should you apply? One might suggest this simple questionnaire:

(1)   Does your subject justify a book, or another book if others already exist? (Subject matter is discussed in chapter 1.)

(2)   Would you have the determination to complete research on all aspects of the subject (including those that might least interest you personally) and to stick at the task of committing the material to paper?

(3)   Have you a basic ability to write? (If you cannot write a letter without a struggle, you will obviously find authorship trying.)

(4)   Are you sure your aims are sensible (that you are not, for instance, convinced that the world is waiting for your new economic theory that will result in immediate peace and prosperity everywhere)?

(5)   Are you willing to be guided, and perhaps to adapt your approach, if a publisher thought that a change would open up a wider market?

If you answer these questions in the affirmative, there is little to stop you, and the task will probably prove less severe than you imagine. Enjoy yourself, and do not be discouraged by relations or friends who hint that your qualifications are inadequate.

1   Subject Matter and Approach

WITH PUBLICATION IN MIND

THE SUREST WAY of writing a book that will not be published is to choose the wrong subject. That no commercial publisher will accept a text on the history of your central heating system, or a manual on methods of cutting bread and butter, is obvious. Yet it is almost as certainly a waste of time to pick a potentially-promising subject and handle it irrationally. Not just the basic subject, but the whole balance of subject matter and the approach to it, require careful thought and planning.

The belief that 'authors should write what they want' is irrelevant where non-fiction is concerned. Those who want to communicate with an audience necessarily hope to see their work *published*. Therefore they cannot entirely ignore the public's taste. They cannot ignore it even if they hope to influence it. However small the audience a writer has in mind, he must try to meet its needs, envisaging the use that potential readers could have for the book, and avoiding putting them off by including an unsuitable range of contents or by unnecessarily flouting publishing conventions. This holds true even if he is not in the least concerned with financial reward; he still has something to communicate and should be serving the interests of his readers.

Be honest about your objective in writing. Those who do it purely for their own amusement can set down what they choose without disciplined shape or scope. This can be an enjoyable occupation, like taking family snapshots or doing the occasional amateur painting. But do not pretend you are merely amusing yourself when in fact you have a wider audience in mind; or, if you are merely amusing yourself, do not blame the publishers who ultimately reject your work. Of course some creative writing may be eminently suitable for publication even though originally done purely for pleasure or in self-expression: some of the best children's stories began with a one-child audience; some novelists who became international figures cared little whether their work was published or not. But such spontaneous achievement is rare; most successful authors plan and execute their work with businesslike practicality, making every effort to put themselves in the reader's place. The chances are that if you want to see your words in print you will have to accept conventions—and accept that the plotting of words on paper is not automatically a form of pure art immune from commercial considerations.

This book is anyway primarily concerned with factual works, which account for an ever-growing proportion of the ever-increasing number of titles published each year. No anti-fiction bias should of course be inferred. Fiction will remain an indispensable means of communication and enrichment; even while writing this chapter a modern novel has been my background reading. But in the past there has been an artificial identification of 'writing' with writing fiction: if your friends heard you were writing a book they assumed it was a novel. In his book *The Truth About Publishing*, published as long ago as 1926, Sir Stanley Unwin complained about the automatic assumption that all books were fiction, and this tendency remains remarkably strong even today.

THE SUBJECT

The best subjects are those that come naturally—subject first and then the desire to write a book. Your professional work or your job may have brought you specialised knowledge of some aspect of your own field; you may be interested in the local canal, have delved into its history, amassed facts about it and the traffic it carried, and ended with a longing to communicate your enthusiasm to others, to provide them with the book you would have loved to read had it existed earlier.

Maybe your hobby is a specialist branch of gardening or astronomy, gastronomy or photography, and you have practical advice that could be useful to others. You may have studied the works of specialists on an aspect of history or scientific research, philosophy or theology, and wish to make a synthesis of their findings in a broader-based book for a wider audience; you may have had the opportunity for some original research in laboratory or field, or to study documentary or other evidence which sheds new light on matters of interest to others. Or you may have travelled to a distant part of the world and have some topical or personal impressions worth sharing.

Many of us have at least one book in us, but anyone with a vague wish to write without any information to impart to any particular audience would be better employed in reading—and living—until a subject and an audience can be defined. So many who have the germ of a book in them fail to work out who the readers are likely to be (or whether they exist) and to orientate the work to please and interest them. The commonest mistakes in approach might be summarised thus:

(1)　Being interested in writing only about what is already known personally or can be discovered easily, and thus failing to produce a viable subject coverage.

(2)　Though coming closer to producing a viable subject coverage, marring it by giving unbalanced vent to some theory, love or hatred.

(3)　Being unable to select a good balance of material and, for instance, floundering when trying to put a local or limited subject in broader perspective, or giving too much minute detail and not enough general picture.

(4)　Skimping the job, to speed publication and financial return, especially by failing to complete research on certain aspects.

Given the right command of subject knowledge, the writing of a book is not necessarily a difficult task. But it must be remembered that books are expensive to produce, and the purchaser paying perhaps several pounds expects something more for his money than is provided by the daily paper or weekly

B

magazine that costs only coppers. Whereas in his newspaper or magazine he is probably satisfied with a fairly superficial and ephemeral coverage, plus perhaps odd items that he might clip out for later use, he will normally expect a book to have lasting value. He also expects it to hang together as a whole with adequate purpose and planning. For this very reason few collections of newspaper articles make satisfactory books— unless they are completely rewritten and reshaped, filling in any gaps.

Before you start writing, therefore, make sure that what you have to say warrants the expensive operation of book production. The obvious question is too frequently overlooked: would you yourself, or would your relations or friends with similar interests, be prepared to pay the conventional price of a hardback book to read what you have to say? Note the word hardback, since few works are issued as cheap paperbacks until they have first made good in hardback form.

Perhaps the manuscripts that publishers are most tired of receiving are personal memoirs. So many people want to start writing about themselves: yourself is, after all, the subject closest to you. It is an easy subject since it requires little if any research; you may come close to complete accuracy, and if you do not, probably no one will know. There is only one snag: generally other people will not find your life and thoughts, once presented in cold print, as all-absorbing as you may do. Like all publishers, my own firm receives an enormous number of unsolicited manuscripts of a strictly personal nature. They come not from famous people, but from ordinary men and women—the story of my personal travels on the Continent, my life in the army and what I have done since, how I came to take over my rival's business, how I live with my husband, how we converted a farmhouse together, how I solved the mystery of the universe, what we think about this, that and the other. People even offer manuscripts interpreting their own dreams.

By no means all this flood of paper is totally uninteresting,

but very few of the manuscripts have sufficient value as a whole
to warrant publication in hardback form at the inevitable high
price. The best manuscripts in this personal category are of
course by those whose lives and experiences really have been
outstanding and are therefore genuinely worth communcat-
ing in detail, or by those who (while using their personal experiences as the book's backbone) concentrate on objective details,
for instance giving plenty of hard practical advice for others
while telling of their difficulties in converting a henhouse into
a holiday cottage. Conversely, the utterly unpublishable manuscripts are by those who lack all modesty—or is it judgement?
Does the engine driver who might perhaps find an interested
audience for accounts of his work on the footplate really expect
readers also to want to hear about his work as sidesman at
the local church, how he cooked his Christmas turkey and his
views on modern youth?

Personal and family jokes and experiences seldom stand up
to presentation to the wide world. Have you never been bored
by a friend's display of his holiday photographs—and he, after
all, is someone you know? Of course generalisations are danger-
ous, and a few reminiscences will always appear in the best-
seller lists, but if you want to see your first book published
you will probably be wise to make it as impersonal as possible,
treating an objective subject in an objective way.

An industrialist wrote a good manuscript on the rise of his
own industry but included quantities of irrelevant personal
matter. Such was his role in the growth of the industry that he
was probably the only person qualified to tell the complete
story, and the use of the personal pronoun and of personal
touches had to be fairly extensive. But never was a man more
incredulous than he was at being told that though people would
be interested in his working life because of the light it shed
on the story of the industry concerned, they would not want
all the odds and ends of information about his religious beliefs
or his children's escapades. His publisher tried to persuade
him to scrap this and instead fill in the earlier history of his

industry which he did not know at first hand and had therefore omitted. 'I cannot believe that people will be more interested in how —— was first manufactured than in my life details,' he said.

So try to place yourself in strangers' shoes and be as objective as possible. If you do have some personal material that will, even in cold print, interest the wide world, wrap it up and put it in its proper context. Thus, while part of the narrative may come easily from memory, you will probably be involved in research to complete the picture. And that, indeed, is the case with most books. It is generally only the superficial sketch that can be written from start to finish without some checking or research.

While other people can write about themselves, and publishers are daily inundated with autobiographies, personal travel tales and the like, you may have it in your power to write the only book on a particular aspect of a factual subject. Such a book may appear to be very specialist and limited in appeal, but if it is the only one it will command a fairly high price (perhaps twice as much per page as an autobiography) and it should have a long life, perhaps being reprinted every few years for a couple of decades. It is often these quiet, solid books of reference value, those that perhaps take the longest to research and write, that live longest and pay the most handsome dividends in the end.

THE APPROACH AND COVERAGE

As well as undertaking research on the less familiar aspects of his subject, an author does need to bring enthusiasm to the task of making his coverage as complete as possible. Forgetting all about finance, the work should be *editorially viable*. It should set out to cover fully a rational subject span, even though this will involve the author in dealing with some matters that he does not find as interesting as others. With the general rise in education standards, and indeed with the increase in the number of non-fiction titles being published, a book must have an adequate raison d'être. Tastes are becoming ever more sophisticated, and there is little room now for the often ill-assembled hotchpotches that were accepted in the earlier years of the century.

Let us go back to the first example in this chapter, that of a person absorbed by the history of his local canal. Between the wars such canal books as were published consisted largely of personal accounts of cruises, interviews with canal personalities, observations on engineering works and odd bits and pieces of history that could be readily gleaned, all put together in a continuous narrative with personal material which often had scant relevance to the canal itself. Some such works were not without charm, and some include information which remains useful to this day. But they were poorly planned, and little if any attempt was made at a definitive, all-round account of any particular aspect, leave alone the whole history of a waterway. Neither the author nor the publisher exercised much discipline; generally publishers then rejected such books outright or accepted them just as they stood.

Today's canal writer will have to be far more systematic in his approach. He will probably gather the material for the basic skeleton in a matter of weeks or months, but considerable application over a long period will be needed to clothe it with the details of what it cost to build the canal, how remarkable or conventional its engineering works were for the period concerned, when exactly it was opened, what kinds of traffic it used to carry and for whom, how much the tolls yielded, when and why the company went bankrupt or was taken over by a competing railway. He will have to search for and study books and records in libraries and record offices, and also carefully search for evidence on the ground. His task will not be complete until he has tapped and synthesised all possible sources of information.

Moreover, even when he has covered all aspects of the chosen canal itself, he will have to make sure he knows enough about neighbouring canals and railways that may have affected the traffic, and perhaps about a local industry whose sudden collapse made the canal close too; and he will still have to make sure he can tell the story with adequate regional and national perspective. On the one hand he must not write up the history of his single canal as though water transport were unique to his corner of the country; on the other, he must discover in just what ways this canal differed from others, so that he does not tire readers—who may know more about canals as a whole than he does—with laborious details of operation common to all. And if he is not prepared to do all this, it is better that he does not attempt the task at all—or at any rate does not expect publication in hardback form. It is no use for him to offer a pot-pourri of just what happens to interest him personally, though within reason certain aspects or periods will probably be given more thorough coverage than others.

Many subjects are more difficult to define than the history of a canal, and different people may well justify covering different segments of material. But the point about editorial viability still holds. A book should set out to cover some rationally-defined subject or segment of it, and do it thoroughly. To take an extreme example, there may be a case for dealing only with the earlier history of a city, or perhaps only with the later history, but you cannot rationally justify covering 1066 to 1850 and 1900 to 1960 on the grounds that the Victorians 'did not do anything'. If you write a book on an English county, you may possibly produce some justification for barely mentioning an extreme area adjoining the next county but you cannot ignore a large town in the middle because you do not happen to like it or know anything about it (though once a book on Somerset did manage to get itself published without any reference, even in the index, to Weston-super-Mare, by far the largest seaside town).

You can of course exercise a balanced personal preference. You can pause in close-up on an aspect that happens to appeal strongly. You can admit that you are giving only a broad outline of another aspect which has perhaps been covered better by another book. You may be able to change the whole purpose of the book originally envisaged so as to make it editorially viable: for instance, if you find that you want to devote three-quarters of a book on Wales to its literary history and associations, then why not plainly make it and label it a book on Welsh literary history. If you are only interested in a certain aspect of a bigger subject, it is often best to define that area and keep to it; this at least will mean that you do not offer a publisher an apparently wider-ranging book which he rejects because its subject coverage is unbalanced.

Even if the whole aim of your book is to put forward some particular viewpoint or theory, a sensible subject range is still essential. While you will naturally make the best of such material as supports your contention, you will only weaken your case if you deny the existence of counter-evidence. In all works where the author's personal view is being projected, it pays to make abundantly plain what is being offered as objective fact and what is personal interpretation. It is too easy to overstate the case even if you do not tamper with the actual evidence, and the reader's confidence may be harder to regain than it was to lose.

As tastes become more sophisticated, in all ways greater care must be taken to prevent inadvertently insulting the reader's intelligence. Fortunately these days few authors resort to slices of imaginary dialogue to cover up a lack of fact, but some are not above indulging in guesswork where the factual evidence is not readily available, and others still introduce irrelevant padding. Topographical works have been among the worst offenders here; until the 1950s many were just scissors-and-paste compilations stuck together with the author's comments on anything under the sun. Two points might usefully be made about them. Firstly, many were designed only for light reading and entertainment, and in days of cheap book production there was an adequate market to make such ephemera commercially worthwhile. Today, however, people obtain their entertainment more cheaply in other ways—such as looking at television, reading the free colour supplements that come with the week-end newspapers and buying paperbacks. (The price difference between a new topographical book making its first appearance in hardback and a paper-covered reprint of popular fiction and other proved successes is far greater now than a generation ago.) Then, secondly, so much topography was of so poor a quality that many younger people dismissed the subject as a whole as being of little interest to them until a new generation of more purposeful works began appearing.

Many new authors are puzzled about how to present their material when a previous book covering basically the same subject is already on the market. The proper answer is surely that a good work should always be complete, self-contained. It may refer the reader to more specialist tomes to discover more detail on certain facets, but a new book is invalidated if the reader is expected to consult a previous work in order to be able to understand and appreciate it. Like most points in this chapter, this may seem obvious: if you are claiming that your new book is more useful than the heavy-going works that have preceded it, do not get out of covering a difficult aspect of the subject by saying that one of these predecessors does it better. Only the reader who wants to range deeper or wider than the context of your book allows should be referred to other works.

CHECK BEFORE YOU START

Certainly before you start writing you should check what other books exist on the same subject. Most publishers have had experience of authors writing in ignorance of the literature already available. There may well be room for another volume, but at least you should know what has gone before and consider how your contribution can be different and better.

If you know a librarian or anyone at an institution which might use your book, or members of the profession or followers of the hobby for whom the work is intended, it may be useful to discuss your basic plan at an early stage, and to note special requirements for reference material, illustrations, length and price. Certain types of book have conventionally to be published at fairly low prices, which limits their length and therefore their scope, and this may make you realise you are undertaking the impossible—or perhaps have two books instead of one. Incidentally, the librarian's or another expert's views on any previous books on the same subjects can be useful. Maybe previous authors omitted or over-emphasised certain aspects; or maybe you will learn that a previous book stands in such high esteem that there is little point in proceeding along the lines you had first fixed.

But do not be downcast when you hear that someone else has almost finished writing the book you are planning. Very many more books are planned than written; many more are started than finished; many more are finished than published; and many more are published than really succeed in their aim. You might be unlucky, but statistically it is likely that the threatened opposition will not materialise, or that the book will in fact be quite different from yours. Probably your rival has been on the point of finishing (or starting?) for the past five years.

There is one further thing you should do before you start the actual writing: plan the book in detail and make sure that you can tackle all the material that has to be included to give proper subject coverage. That does not necessarily mean collecting all the material before you make a beginning; but you need to know that it does exist and is accessible to you, and that you are capable of absorbing and synthesising it. A short synopsis is essential. It may consist of only a dozen or so headings scribbled on a cigarette packet or scrap of newsprint, but it will prove surprisingly useful. Quite apart from the fact that an assessment of the overall plan will make for easier and more orderly writing once you start, it will pinpoint weaknesses in your approach and material. It may make you realise that unless you devote your next holiday to research on a particular point in a certain record office, the execution of the whole book will be delayed. It may even make you realise that you are attempting the impossible, resulting in your cutting down the scope or turning to a different subject.

Some subjects are inevitably difficult to handle; before you commit yourself to the project, perhaps invite the interest of a publisher and tell your colleagues and friends of your plan; make sure you can bring it off. A high credibility rating is one of the author's strongest assets; do not lose it at the beginning of your literary career by announcing things you cannot accomplish. You will sink even in your own estimation and that of your wife (or husband) who in all probability will have much to bear while you are 'in labour'.

THE TITLE

Most people also like to decide on a title before starting. A good, clear, telling title is more important than it used to be. This again is partly because tastes have become more sophisticated, and today an oblique or obscure title for a non-fiction book usually seems as naïve as a piece of imagined conversation devised to 'make the book more interesting'. It is also partly because with the increasing avalanche of new books it becomes ever harder for booksellers and librarians to digest and remember new titles, and the more contrived the title the less likely it is to register.

Some books defy a nice neat title. If you cannot adequately convey the scope of the work in the title proper, try a combination of a short, snappy title and a longer, descriptive subtitle (such as this book has). If you cannot succeed in labelling the work even then, should you be writing it at all? Should its structure and aim be simplified? If you cannot describe it briefly, how will others do so? Remember that advertising space is expensive, and your publisher will not be able to afford an essay to describe your book's basic aims in the press, even if the public would read it. There are many well-known exceptions, but generally the book that is difficult to describe is also difficult to sell.

The title may be changed and improved along the route . . . but at least establish the possibility of finding a suitable label before you commit yourself to writing a book.

WHAT IS YOUR MARKET?

Just as you define your subject, you must define your market. The main one is probably fairly obvious, but without jeopardising your book's success there, can you do anything to widen the appeal? The result could be to double your sales and your number of readers.

For example, can an academic book on say a scientific subject be written and presented so that it will also appeal to more amateur scientists without damaging the work's academic standards? The avoidance of technical jargon, and the weaving in of odd explanations to help the uninitiated in a way that will not offend experts who already know, will go a long way to help. If you have a wider audience in mind, take care to avoid a display of the fact that you know far more than the reader. Do not assume he knows previous works on the same subject, and if referring to these do so by title as well as by author—eg 'As Smith says in his *Basic Elements*' is kinder to the non-specialist reader than just 'According to Smith'. If there is a possibility of a fairly wide general sale, it can also be sensible to consolidate the footnotes at the end of the book, with adequate cross-referencing between them and the text; some non-academic readers—and bookshop managers—are discouraged by the presence of a large number of notes mixed in with the text. But if your interest in writing the book is solely to raise your status in the academic world, you may want to follow the traditional academic practices in these matters and not worry about possible lost sales—providing your publisher does not mind the lost sales either.

The requirements of general and specialist readers can often be partially reconciled by concentrating certain specialist and very technical information into tables, appendices or self-contained paragraphs which can be skipped by those not interested. Adequate headings and general signposting can also do a lot to render a specialist book intelligible to the layman.

Then, are you writing for adults or for children? Especially in fields like popular science and natural history, the division is far less sharp than it used to be, and it is often possible to combine both markets by using simple, direct language, sticking to the point and explaining technical terms—in an unpatronising kind of way. No playing-down is required for the juvenile reader (his powers of comprehension in scientific and natural history matters are anyway often greater than assumed). Diagrams and pictures can obviously help, as again can the consolidation of optional-extra technical material into self-contained paragraphs, tables and appendices. Many educational textbooks are today presented as straightforwardly as standard adult non-fiction titles and can therefore be published in trade editions for sale through bookshops as well as in special textbook editions for school and college use.

Then, are you writing for a local, national or international audience? Widening the scope here can dramatically increase sales. Taking the example of a history of a single town, if you concentrate entirely on local matters, dutifully chronicling the doings of local bigwigs, with lists of mayors and councillors, the history can only serve people with some concentrated interest in that town. If, however, you project your town as an example of similar places throughout the country, or a part of the country, and show how it fits into regional or national trends, how it was affected by outside influences and what influence it had on general trade and commerce, there will be at least a small market elsewhere.

In the case of books of regional interest, the larger the region the greater the potential sale, not merely because the book will then cover an area of greater population and more bookshops, but because the wider scope may open up a stronger national and even international market. Thus a book on whisky-distilling in Scotland would have an American sale in the way that a book on whisky-distilling in North East Scotland would not. Or need your regional book be a regional one at all? For instance, a manuscript on *Growing Rarer Shrubs and Trees in South West England* was readily convertible into *Growing Rarer British Shrubs and Trees*. Most of the shrubs and trees could, the author realised, be grown in at least the milder parts of Britain other than the South West, and even in cooler areas some gardeners will risk trying rarer species. A book with 'South West England' in its title might never gain a national circulation.

Widening the interest still further, can the book appeal to a substantial overseas as well as home market? This is where the greatest reward may be obtained. Very many British books have a potential American and other overseas sale, but this is frequently lost. Sometimes it is lost because the author failed to include some American material that would have helped promote the book across the Atlantic, or because he failed to check his American or Australian facts as carefully as his British ones. Occasionally American prospects are thrown away by an author going out of his way to be anti-American or generally xenophobic. More often authors simply fail to appreciate the possibilities of overseas sales, drawing all their examples from Britain and introducing place names, slang terms and money sums that can only be understood by the British reader. Adaption of a few dozen sentences might render a book acceptable overseas, but once the work has been published the opportunity for a special American edition may have been reduced. Think big, remember in what parts of the world English is spoken, and do not put unnecessary obstacles in the way of international circulation. Translation is a different matter, since a translated book has to be set up in type afresh and adjustments can be made at that stage; but if an American publisher is willing to co-operate after seeing the manuscript or proofs, the British publisher will often print (or run-on) an American edition at the same time as his own.

THE QUANTITY OF FACT

A non-fiction book does not have to be wholly solemn, let alone characterless; even though you may use the personal pronoun sparingly, quite a bit of your character may emerge incidentally. The work may be fun to write and fun to read. But never be ashamed of keeping to the facts. The dramatised-documentary approach is usually less telling than the straightforward documentary. Unless you are a Thornton Wilder (in which case you are unlikely to be discouraged by anything said here), you will make the history of your real town sound a great deal more interesting and convincing than that of an imaginary one. But what you do, do thoroughly; even in narrow selfish terms, twice the labour may bring you three times the income and respect. One accepted standard work is worth many potboilers.

One other point is worth making. Writing a specialist book can be a lonely business, since few of your relatives or friends may be able to comprehend it or its aims. The temptation to please friends and relatives by taking their advice to make the work less technical and more easily digestible is real; but remember that they are probably not the kind of people who would ever go out and buy or borrow that type of book. They are not your market. Forget them and stick to writing for the people who share your kind of interest and will positively pay for reading your work. If the book sells steadily through successive editions, your esteem will rise among your acquaintances even if they have not the foggiest idea what it is all about, what could have made you write it—or why other people read it.

2 The Mechanics of Writing

PLANNING

FOR PEOPLE WHO come to authorship because they have something specific they want to communicate, and not because they want to exercise the art of communication for its own sake, the actual writing of the book can be a wearisome business. Each author has to discover largely through trial and error what methods suit him best. Indeed, writing is such an individual matter that at first it might seem merely fatuous to chatter brightly on how best to set about it. There are, however, certain broad avenues of approach which help reduce frustration and wasted labour.

It undoubtedly helps to begin by appreciating that the process of committing original material to paper is demanding. It tends, moreover, to make demands on your family as well as yourself: not only may you be tired and irritable after a writing session, but you may have to curtail the family's noise-making, have time for fewer outings, and make everyone in the house acutely aware that you are at work.

Most experienced writers like to keep the agony to the minimum by making a clear-cut distinction between the time spent on research and planning before writing, or on revision afterwards, and the actual creative period in the middle. Too many part-time authors go to their desk on a Friday evening or a Sunday morning without a crisp objective, and waste time in a muddle of mixed tasks. If they kept to a definite plan, they could make life less strained for themselves and those around them, could probably get the job done more quickly—incidentally increasing their earnings—and keep the promised delivery date to the publisher!

While engaged on the central creative task of committing your material to paper, you will be fully stretched. The job genuinely requires an unusually tense discipline and concentration—and especially if you are not used to the art of communication, nothing is more discouraging than the sight of blank pieces of paper that somehow you have to fill. When you are 'in labour', you may justifiably regard yourself as a maestro commanding three times your ordinary hourly rate of pay. But once this superman has been engaged, do not toy with minor details of research that can be added later in more relaxed mood. If during these periods of highly-concentrated work you are helped by being spoiled with music, unlimited quantities of luxurious copy paper, coffee or whatever, then indulge yourself—provided again that all this applies just to the period of creative writing and not to the longer and more mundane periods of research and revision.

It follows that well before you get down to the actual writing sessions, you should not merely have completed your research and have all the material (especially quotations you want to use) available in handy form, but have worked out the book's general plan. Ideally there should be a detailed synopsis allotting all the material to specific chapters, and even quoting the order of ingredients within the individual chapters; but whether you have a formal synopsis which the publisher may have vetted, make do with headings written on a cigarette packet, or merely keep the general scheme at the back of your head, you should know exactly what goes where.

Some people claim that they cannot produce a synopsis and would prefer just to start writing and 'see how things turn out'. Frankly, if you cannot work out a simple preliminary plan of attack, you are unlikely to be a good author. No film company can send off a director on location with the expensive film unit before he has planned what to shoot. Rather than spend valuable creative time on committing material to paper before you have a clear sense of direction, it is probably better to go to the other extreme and set yourself a definite target of how much to write, or what particular aspects to cover, in a given time. At least you are less likely to succumb to distractions, and if your wife knows that you are really hard at work and will have something to show for it, she will find it easier to keep the family temporarily quiet and your friends at bay.

Once under way do anything to avoid interrupting the flow of words. Refuse to become bogged down in the first paragraph: the important thing is to let the narrative start telling itself. The introduction can be considered later. Often enough the first paragraph over which you may have struggled for half a day seems redundant when you finish the chapter: many book chapters, like newspaper articles, are stronger shorn of their concluding sentence or so as well as their introductions, though these may have taken longest to compose.

Leave gaps for any statistical or reference details you suddenly remember are not yet at hand, and do not worry about the odd ugly sentence slipping through. *Keep the narrative on the move*, even at the expense of leaving a line or two of gibberish where you have to explain a ticklish point; once the rest of the chapter is completed it will be much easier to smooth out or entirely rewrite any troublesome passages.

ORDER AND CONTINUITY

Writing sessions need to be as long as possible since the beginning of each session is used on becoming reacclimatised; often three-quarters of the output comes in the last half of the time. Also, pack in as many sessions as you can until a natural break in the book is reached, for continuity is vitally important. From this point of view the easiest books are those with self-contained chapters; providing you can keep continuity within each chapter, gaps between them do not matter. But where a strong continuous thread runs—or should run—through a complete book, as in a closely argued scientific or historical work, the ideal is to live with the work until the whole rough draft is completed. Incidentally, professional journalists are among those who find it hardest to attain continuity; not only are they

c

used to writing self-contained pieces seldom exceeding 1,500 words, but the routine journalistic output which must go on alongside book-writing, with probably erratic working hours, gives a divided loyalty. With honourable exceptions, their books tend to lack sustained writing and to be made up of staccato self-contained sections.

A carefully thought-out synopsis should of course help produce continuity of theme as well as enable you to make the best use of your writing time. Even if you find it easier to write the chapters in a different order from what is finally intended, the synopsis will help control the selection of material to be included or excluded each time. For a variety of reasons it may be easier to start in the middle of the book, and indeed there is much to be said for tackling the easiest chapters first. The difficult portions, perhaps especially the introduction, then tend to look less forbidding when you reach them.

Personally I think that the question of order of contents is so important that a muddle here is the one hitch that should be allowed to halt a creative writing session. I have suggested leaving gaps for missing material, or passing bungled explanations in the rough draft, to enable the writing to be kept on the move. But if the basic order is sliding awry, the trouble of sorting it out later may be worse than that of stopping now. Of course this is a question of degree. If you recall that some fact or argument should have been added at a point you have already passed, it may be best to indicate the fact in the margin and go on. But if you have lost the sense of direction, then stop.

Be logical in the way you present your material. If your order of ingredients is illogical, you will find it hard to carry the reader with you: in his struggle to keep abreast with your main story or argument, he may miss the subtler points; or even worse he may be sidetracked by oddments and lose the main thread. Take care to make plain that a digression is a digression, and if for instance you are dealing with the Tower of London, do not suddenly switch to a potted biography of Judge Jefferies as though he were the book's main subject.

Avoid fragmentation. Do not write down material just as it comes into your head, perhaps resulting in details about the same subject being irrationally peppered throughout long sections of the book. A good synopsis should ensure that the right aspects are thoroughly covered in the right chapters. But make sure that even within individual chapters or paragraphs, the order is logical. For instance, you may slip into an A, B, C, A, B, C pattern, twice working through basically the same sequence, possibly with a slightly different background or argument, but with the same facts relating to A, B and C still appearing in both sequences. Almost invariably logic is better served and space saved if all the matter about A is concentrated in one place before moving on to B.

Sometimes you may want to elaborate on material A to introduce both material B and material C, so that the order becomes A, B, A, C. Even if there is a logical link between A and C, unless you are a skilled and practised writer it will be clearer to concentrate everything to do with A in one place. When you come to introduce material C, you can then either refer back to A or repeat an essential point making clear that it is a repetition. But no additional fact about A should be held back to provide the introduction to C.

If the A-C link seems as vital as the A-B one, you will probably have to accept that you cannot always convey to the reader every nuance of an argument without confusing him. You may be able to establish the additional link elsewhere; but even assuming that your readers have the same degree of comprehension as yourself, the progressions of material need to be as simple as possible, even at the expense of having to drop a supplementary point you would have enjoyed. (You can perhaps add a footnote as an optional extra for those willing to consider finer detail—a note that can be overlooked, at least at first, by readers concentrating on the basic theme.)

A fairly ruthless determination to streamline the progression of fact is particularly necessary when considering the chronological versus the subject approach in books with an historical content. Some of the most disappointing historical manuscripts I have read have been those by authors who could not decide which of these two approaches to adopt and who chopped and changed in mid-stream resulting in inexcusable fragmentation of material.

Personally I am a strong believer in the subject approach, since the strictly chronological one in itself tends to disperse related facts. Take the case of a railway history in which the author has to tell the story of a main line and that of several branch lines having junctions with it. If the chronological approach is adopted, there may be a dozen or more references to the development of any one branch line. Not merely may these references interfere with the flow of the narrative about the main line—and detract from its interest—but the story of the branch line may not come out clearly in its own right. If the subject approach is adopted, the reader's attention will at one point be fully focused on the branch line and there will be a much better chance of describing its history, character, traffic and so on. It may of course be impossible to tell the story of the main line without some reference to the existence of the branch; in that case a suitable supplementary reference (probably quoting the page on which the main description will be found) can be included, but all the main facts about the branch will still be in one place.

Authors can be too reluctant to introduce cross-references to other sections or to repeat an essential item of information in a way that makes plain that it is a repetition; their books lack adequate signposting. There is perhaps a feeling that it insults the reader's intelligence to remind him of some fact he has already been told, but nobody can be offended by a reminder in brackets especially if the author tactfully acknowledges the fact that it is a reminder. For instance: (As I said in Chapter 1, adequate signposting is especially useful when a book is aimed at two markets, perhaps helping laymen or young readers to find their way round a technical work.) What does offend or at least puzzle readers is a lack of clarity, and in particular those hazy circular arguments that suddenly bring you back to your starting point.

Disorderly manuscripts will repeat the same facts, the same sentiments, sometimes the same adjectives, perhaps a couple of pages, perhaps thirty-nine pages, apart. An even worse example is furnished by a basically interesting manuscript being processed in my office while I write this chapter: it repeats virtually the same lengthy paragraph over 100 pages apart, the only variation being in the spelling of a proper name and in the entirely different conclusion! Our editor had to cut the manuscript into pieces to reassemble it in a more rational order, and thus ended with the two sections on the same subject next to each other, different spelling, contradictory conclusion and all.

THE NUMBER OF DRAFTS

New authors often seem unable to decide whether they are likely to need one or more rough drafts before getting the final manuscript typed, and whether the first attempt should be written or typed. Obviously this is entirely a matter for the individual; the only rule is that the copy sent to the publisher should be neatly typed and that (for safety's sake) at least one carbon copy should be taken of this final typing. Very few authors indeed, however, can turn out perfect copy in the right order straight from a typewriter they are having to feed with carbons and flimsy sheets as well as with top-copy paper. So there will be a preliminary draft in some form or other.

Typing is for most people quicker and neater, and if you can translate your thoughts to paper via the machine, so much the better; if your writing output becomes sizeable, you will need to do so. Typewriters and dictaphones are of course accepted as routine tools far more readily than in times past; a generation ago many would have thought it shocking to suggest bypassing the physical chore of handwriting, though actually some famous authors did help popularise the typewriter in literary circles at a very early stage.

When a beginnner, I used to write first drafts of books and newspaper articles in abbreviated longhand; but now I type everything, occasionally pausing to handwrite a particularly complicated sentence. After finishing the first rough draft, with double spacing and generous margins, I revise with a ballpoint pen and perhaps retype any odd sheets that have proved troublesome. This or a second draft, usually produced after a pause in case fresh thoughts occur, is then seen by my wife, who happens to be our firm's editorial director, and after a final joint check the manuscript is typed finally by a secretary.

But everyone has to discover a recipe for himself taking his personal circumstances into account. While I often prefer to work quickly through two preliminary drafts, others may prefer to polish a single draft as they go. For most people, though, it pays to leave a gap between writing the first draft and revising it; if the first chapter drafts are written over a period, to compress your revision into a shorter time may produce better continuity; and if the chapters are produced in a different order from that to be used in the book, it is sensible to revise them in the correct order. But necessary and useful though revision is, you can spend too long at it and if you interfere with your original work (especially your basic factual structure) too much, you may rob it of spontaneity. Whether you write or type the rough draft, it may help to use abbreviations; journalists use a simple t for the, o for of, w for with, tt for that, hv for have, and so on, and leave out vowels in many longer words.

If you write or type on the same standard-sized paper, you can know roughly how many words that sheet accommodates. Many books have to be written to a specified length, and the author who values his time will allocate a rough length to each chapter and make sure that he does not grossly exceed or fall short of it. Up to 10 or 15 per cent of your words may then be lost in polishing and revision without the deletion of actual factual material. Indeed many of the best books are those that have had to be slightly shortened after first writing so that all repetitions and superfluous words are removed. Do not be stingy in supplying yourself with suitable paper. If your time is worth anything at all, it will not pay to use miscellaneous scraps which are hard to file tidily and prevent easy assessment of length. The other day, incidentally, I heard of an author who typed his draft manuscript on the blank back of printed material circulated to him in the Government department where he works. He realised too late, alas, that the information was 'classified' and that he should not even send out the draft for fair-copying!

TYPEWRITERS AND DICTAPHONES

Whether or not you type the rough draft, or indeed even if you have the final copy for the publisher prepared by a professional typist, you will find a typewriter essential. It can be invaluable for notemaking in research; your business letters, including those to your publisher, will look far more professional when your typist may not be available, and you can retype any odd sheets altered after the main typing has been completed. The author who says that he cannot afford to buy, or cannot be bothered to learn to use, a simple portable typewriter has just not arrived. Yet one still comes across engineers and others regularly using advanced equipment in their everyday jobs who fight shy of the typewriter. Of course you will not match your wife's performance if she was a professional secretary before marriage, but anyone who can drive a car, take photographs or even use a vacuum cleaner should be able to master a typewriter using two or four fingers in amateur style within a matter of hours—and even with two fingers a speed much exceeding that of most people's handwriting can quickly be acquired.

One of the larger, more robust portable models at around £50 should, with reasonable care, outlive several cars at over ten times the price, and there are tax savings (see chapter 8). Whether or not you give the machine regular mechanical attention, do not be niggardly over ribbon changes (unless you specifically need the second colour, all-black ribbons of course give best value) and occasionally clean the keys or at least remove the accumulations of dirt which 'fill in' letters such as e, a, and o.

If your wife likes to fair-type your manuscript at the same time as you want to compose fresh copy or write letters or notes, then it is not ludicrous extravagance to buy a second machine, perhaps second-hand. Writing a book is often hard enough without rendering the mechanics unneccessarily difficult. (To quote another example, some authors are continually interrupted by telephone calls for their wives or children having to be taken in the work room, yet do not feel justified in moving the telephone or adding an extension which might cost the equivalent of time spent in producing only half a dozen pages of good copy.)

Many people do not find dictaphones and other recording gadgets so useful, partly because it is genuinely difficult to dictate long continuous passages smoothly while keeping to the point and partly because it is harder to revise and inject new material into what you have said. But some authors find it easiest to break the ice in this way—to get their matter spoken roughly on to tape, then typed, and then revised. Certainly a dictating machine has its uses in research.

POINTS OF ENGLISH

Firstly, most people who consider writing a book at all probably know how to write in some kind of style; they may not completely have forgotten their school English; they will at the very least be used to writing letters. And if they want help there are specialist works on the market.

Secondly, from the publication point of view it curiously matters much less if a writer's English is unpolished than if he cannot sort out his subject range and order of ingredients. Consider the publisher's position. Few of his staff or freelance editors are skilled enough to tear apart a disorderly manuscript on a complicated subject and restore it so that it flows as sweetly as though it had been written with the correct progression of material in the first place. The cost of this skilled work, even if someone can be found to do it, is such that manuscripts needing drastic replanning usually have to be rejected. Compared with that, it is simple enough for a sub-editor to smooth out grammar and clumsy sentences and even to rewrite complete paragraphs, providing the basic planning of the book is satisfactory.

This book is not of course for authors who hope to write literary classics. Most of those writing factual books, using language simply as a tool with which to present the material, should merely do their best. That is not to say that skilled use of language is not important; some strictly factual books are so well written that they are works of pure literature in their own right, and they serve their subject all the better for it. But if your book is full of interesting material, logically presented, a polished command of language is not essential, especially if you find a publisher who sees the virtue of the work as a whole and is prepared to help in giving the final polish.

If there is a hint more useful than all others it is that good writers are those who read widely. If a book can earn the comment 'A well thought-out synthesis resulting from careful research' the author has become a professional. Reading is obviously the essence of research; but it is equally the basis of being able to synthesise, to present a smooth, rounded treatment with good perspective and the wood standing out firmly from the trees. For reading not only teaches the basic facts you need to know about your subject, but the broader background— and of course how to handle the English language with an adequate vocabulary and variety of construction.

Especially if you are a technically-minded person with something to communicate rather than the desire to communicate for its own sake, extend your reading to subjects other than your own. Whether it is a newspaper or a novel, whether you read yourself or your wife reads to you, or you listen to 'Book at Bedtime' on the radio—imbibe, note how other people communicate, get yourself interested in the whole business of conveying fact and argument through the written word.

Your style of writing will be your own. 'Rules' do not matter, but commonsense does. You will, for instance, realise that not everything you have to say is of equal importance, and will seek to develop high spots standing out above the more ordinary parts of the book. As in music, an unvaried pitch or tone becomes tedious. Much can be achieved by careful variation in the length of sentences, using simple ones with a single phrase and more complex ones with several associated statements. Any competent writer avoids overworking a particular construction and especially any personal trick of style; neither diehard traditionalists, writing in nineteenth-century style and employing archaic constructions and phrases, nor pace-setters eager to turn fresh nouns into verbs are easy or convincing to read. Especially on new and technical subjects, a fairly modern style is usually the happiest, adopting some of the contemporary conventions, even at the expense of some of the older grammatical rules, but never relying on jargon or extreme colloquialism.

To have your work read aloud by someone else is a severe but invaluable test: it is the nearest you can get to receiving your message as others will, for familiarity with the written words tends to impair your own impartiality. Once something has been written at all, if it is passable English, it may be taken too much for granted that the words used are the best and that the arguments are convincing. Reading aloud can cruelly show up weak continuity and weak writing.

3 The Physical Book

TECHNICAL LIMITATIONS

MANY AUTHORS would enjoy their work more, and have better relations with their publishers, if they appreciated even a little about the technical limitations of book production, which from many points of view is still a depressingly rough-and-ready process. For those wanting greater detail on printing, binding, illustrations, etcetera, there are specialist works available. Here the aspects of production immediately relevant to the writer are discussed; this is where his own influence for good or bad will be most felt by the publisher and printer. At the beginning, when you consider what your finished book will look like and those who will buy it, it helps to bear in mind a couple of well-proven facts that publishers and booksellers have to live with.

Perhaps the most difficult to credit is that a large proportion of the book-buying public judge value for money partly in terms of physical bulk, especially the book's thickness. That this should be so in an age of small homes and limited shelf room is perhaps as surprising as it is regrettable, but it is undeniably true. Increasingly book-buyers are prepared to pay a good price for a specialist work with reference value, but with very few exceptions (such as the ultra-technical manual) this price has to be backed up by physical bulk. Purchasers have to be made to feel justified in spending their money, and that an expensive work must be dressed up to look like one. So the fact that a book with 350 well-filled pages represents good value at a certain price is unfortunately not recognised if the paper is so thin (no matter how high the quality) that the physical bulk is less than that of many books of 200 pages.

If this sounds absurd, make sure that you yourself do not

sometimes take the same line, being shocked by the high price of a book that appears smaller than it is. The point was once brought forcibly home to me when I was browsing in a book-shop and saw a couple examine a book published by my own firm—a reference work of over 600 pages priced at £3. It represented excellent value for money, but we had made the mistake of assuming that (because it had proven reference value) we could ignore the conventional bulk consideration; we had used a thin but high-quality paper similar to that found in many Bibles. 'What a nerve,' was the husband's comment to the woman when they spotted the price. And these were not people who would balk at paying £3 for a book anyway; they went on to find a £4 book on a similar subject containing fewer pages but printed on a thicker, rougher paper and *looking* altogether a larger work—another of our books as it happened, which is why the incident has stuck in my mind. They bought without further hesitation.

Remember, too, that the publisher has first to sell books to booksellers. If the booksellers feel they look too small for their price, copies may never reach bookshop shelves in quantities adequate to ensure a good initial circulation. And even if the specialist reader feels that a book represents good value, he may—in practice—have to justify the expenditure to his wife. It goes against the grain to pay more for an article than it appears to be worth. A professor once gave his wife the price of a book he required urgently and which she offered to buy while in town shopping; though she knew the need for the work and its price, she was unprepared for what struck her as its bad value since it was printed on thin paper and—unable to bring herself to make the purchase—sheepishly went home without it.

Many authors will say that all this is ridiculous. Perhaps most of us in the trade have felt like that ourselves at some time. But experience proves that there is virtually only one exception to the rule about bulk or thickness: with picture books printed on high-class art paper, which does not bulk much but weighs heavy, people are prepared to judge value for money on a weight basis instead! Otherwise only extremely technical works are exempt: manuals bought simply as essential tools, books that would have to be bought whatever the price and format.

Another popular fallacy is that publishers could reduce the price of many books by issuing them in paperback form instead of as hardbacks. Many an author has protested to his publisher that £3 sounds far too much for his new book and could not it be made £1 in a cheaper format. The answer is almost certainly no. Paperbacks are normally cheap for one of two reasons. Either they are produced in prodigious quantities, in the case of proven successes, and the sheer scale of the operation brings down the unit price. Or the sheets are printed at the same time as those for the hardback edition, the cost of typesetting, blockmaking and so on being charged against the more expensive hardback copies.

Most non-fiction books will have a first print order of only 2,500 to 5,000 copies; not enough revenue to pay the high cost of typesetting will be generated unless the first edition appears in hardback form at the conventional fairly high hardback price—and nor will the author be adequately rewarded for his effort. The actual costs of producing a paperback are not vastly less than those of producing a hardback; it is not the binding case that really makes the difference. A binding case may indeed cost only coppers more per copy than a paper cover for an edition of 3,000 or 4,000. If therefore you suggest to your publisher that he produces your work at £1 in paper covers instead of at £3 as a hardback, you may be saving him only $2\frac{1}{2}$ per cent of his costs yet reducing his income (and yours) by two-thirds. This of course assumes that the same number of copies are sold, and in fact a paperback at £1 is still so relatively expensive that it may not sell any more readily than a hardback at £3. The point has been made elsewhere that it is well to ignore the reactions of friends and relatives to your book's price: they are usually unlikely purchasers, whether at £3 hardback or £1 paperback.

Right the way through the trade people expect hardbacks to be expensive and paperbacks to be cheap, and they expect all but the most popular new books, those that will sell in tens of thousands, first to appear as hardbacks, to enable their publishers to recoup the costs of typesetting and blockmaking quickly, and to enable their authors to gain a fair return. Paperback sales must be regarded as the extras earned by successful books. Sometimes certain types of book are published simultaneously as hardbacks and paperbacks, but even so the paperback sales should be regarded largely as extra ones—for in fact public libraries and other institutions, and also many private buyers, will still prefer the hardback form with its greater durability.

A separate word should perhaps be said about educational books. Many are produced exclusively for classroom use, and may be produced in paperback form (in very large numbers of course) or as hardbacks using cheap materials and without jackets. But the boundary between educational and non-educational books is becoming blurred, many works written as school texts eventually having a general sale in a conventional 'trade' edition at a higher price. The author will receive far more royalty per copy from the trade edition than from the educational one.

LETTERPRESS OR LITHO

Most books are printed in one of two ways: letterpress (from metal type) or offset lithography. Letterpress is normally used for short-run books (say up to 5,000 copies) because its initial costs are cheaper. Lithography is used for long-run books, such as popular annuals and many textbooks, and for reprints of old books (where the existing type has been melted and it is cheaper to reproduce the work photographically from a copy of an earlier edition than set it up afresh). Lithography also allows half-tone illustrations to be combined with the text on a roughish or matt-surface paper; while using a paper that bulks well, to make the book thick enough, you can place the photographs anywhere you like in the book, close to the text to which they refer. But against these advantages, the quality of litho black-and-white photographs seldom reaches that obtained with letter-press blocks.

Most books being written by the authors to whom this work is addressed will be of a semi-specialist nature, and being new books most will be printed by letterpress. That means that the photographs will have to be printed on a smooth-surfaced, glossy art paper, and here is the weakness of the letterpress method: though the quality of the photographs will normally be higher than if lithography was used, they have to be con-fined to plate pages, or else the whole book has to be on art paper. The use of art paper throughout is unsatisfactory from several points of view. The art paper is expensive, and far from ideal for continuous reading since it tends to reflect the light and weary the eyes; many of the type faces designed for book work cannot indeed be used on so hard a surface. Art paper also has little bulk, giving a thin, if heavy, book.

The alternative of using two kinds of paper is therefore usually adopted where the text is of greater importance than the illustrations. An extremely wide range of papers suitable for continuous reading is available, and they are made in a variety of bulks: the publisher could produce books of 100, 200 or 300 pages all to the same finished bulk. But if the pictures have to be printed on separate art paper, they cannot then be placed beside the text to which they refer.

THE PLATES IN LETTERPRESS BOOKS

Perhaps three-quarters of the authors consulting this work will see their first (or next) book printed letterpress with one paper for the text and another for the plates, so let us see what difficulties and technical considerations are involved.

The commonest book size in Britain and America today is demy octavo, giving a finished page size of $8\frac{1}{2}$ by $5\frac{1}{2}$ inches. Most printers print this and other similar sizes in what is known as quad form, that is to say in four sections of 16 pages on one sheet, 64 pages in all, or 32 pages on each side of the sheet. Printers and publishers know their 16-times table: tell a publisher that a manuscript is making 177 printed pages, and he will immediately see what he can do to take out one page, reducing it to 176, or an 'even working'. The most economical book is one whose text pages total a multiple of 16, if not of 32. Cheap novels must usually be produced to give an even working, which can of course be achieved by slightly varying the amount of type (the number of lines or the length of lines) on each page, or the space allocated for headings at the beginnings of chapters. In the case of more specialist, expensive works, an exact even working is not so essential, though it will be arranged wherever possible, and authors are often asked to help by cutting out an odd page or two—usually surprisingly easy—or even by supplying an extra page.

Though printed in 64-page sheets, most books are bound in 16-page sections, for the pages on the large sheet are imposed in such a way that when each is folded and guillotined it makes, as it were, four booklets of 16 pages each. (Some cheaper books, or long books using thin paper, are bound in 32-page sections.) If the half-tone plates are printed on separate art pages, they can either be wrapped round or inserted in the middle of these 16-page sections. The most common practice is to wrap them round the second, fourth, sixth and so on 16-page section, so that one sheet (two pages) of half-tones comes between every 16 pages of text, and every half-tone page is opposite a text page. But some variation is of course necessary if the proportion of picture to text pages is too great. In that event, as well as the wrap-rounds, some pictures can be inserted in the middle of 16-page sections (in which case there will be four pages of pictures together, the middle two pages facing each other and not facing text pages); or there may be complete 16-page sections of half-tones, which is cheaper but tends to give book-buyers the impression that the book is not so well illustrated as when the pictures are distributed throughout the work. Indeed, a book with 32 pages of plates all placed together often *looks* less plentifully illustrated than one with only 16 pages well distributed. Most people like flicking through for pictures and finding them occurring every now and then to break up the text.

Because by its very nature it does not fall either at the beginning or in the middle of a 16-page text section, the frontispiece (facing the title page) cannot be bound in with the other art pages in an economical, conventional manner, but has to be tipped-in by hand. This is an expensive method. In bygone days it used to be employed extensively to place pictures on art paper opposite the text to which they referred, but costwise it is now out of the question; the finished result is anyway less neat, the tipped-in pages sometimes working loose.

Frontispieces are therefore expensive to bind—and expensive to print, since they cannot be part of an economical working of half-tones. If a book has 16 pages of half-tones plus the frontispiece, the frontispiece has to be machined separately. If a book has 12 pages of plates plus a frontispiece, the frontispiece can be machined with the plates but an eighth of the total sheet of paper will then be cut to waste. Fold a piece of typing paper three times, or to put it another way, fold it into eight so that eight 'pages' are to view on each side, and you will see that each quarter of the sheet can make a four-page section, two pages to view on each side of the sheet. If the frontispiece has to be taken out of this sheet, it will be printed on one side only of half of one of these quarter sections. So the frontispiece is not only expensive but tends to give poor value for money; you may find your publisher can more easily be persuaded to allow you another four pages of plates instead, that is 16 instead of 12, so that full use is made of a 16-page section of art paper (all four quarters of our folded piece of typing paper).

Publishers who take the production of their books seriously will decide well in advance where the half-tones are to be placed, and will take care to prevent maps or any other line illustrations printed on the text paper appearing opposite them, since their appearance might clash. Also, if all the half-tone pages are to appear opposite text pages, it will be possible to print the captions of the illustrations at the foot of the text pages, so that the blocks can occupy the whole of the expensive art paper, and the captions can be long if required.

Long captions may be useful additions, for the very reason that the pictures will not (except by luck) appear beside the text to which they refer. Book production is indeed rough-and-ready, but if authors realise the limitations they can at least make the best of them. Where you have separate text and art paper, you are in effect running two books simultaneously; the photographs and the text will probably follow the same basic subject order, but they will not exactly keep pace with each other, and adequate cross-referencing between text and picture pages is necessary.

OTHER COST CONSIDERATIONS FOR ILLUSTRATIONS

Curiously, though buyers of many kinds of non-fiction books expect a fair modicum of illustrations, they are not necessarily prepared to pay more for a large number. In the assessment of a book's value, plate pages frequently seem to be regarded as an optional extra—there must be a reasonable minimum, but anything above that tends not to be taken into account. So the publisher may offer the author the use of up to 16 pages of plates but remain reluctant to go further, since he might not safely be able to raise the book's price to cover 24, 32 or 48 pages.

There are probably several reasons why the plates tend to be disregarded in the value for money assessment. The plate pages themselves add little to the bulk of a book. For instance, another 64 pages of plates in this book would make it surprisingly little thicker, and if the price were doubled (as it would probably have to be, to cover the high costs of blocks, art paper and plate printing) it would appear poor value. And usually plate pages are not numbered in consecutively with the text pages. At the head of its main reviews, *The Times Literary*

Supplement quotes the number of pages in a book, but this is the highest folio number to be found—the number of the last page. It usually excludes the plates, and if the number of plate pages is high in relation to the number of text pages, the yardstick is obviously misleading. Today some publishers arrange one consecutive numbering sequence throughout their books, taking in preliminary pages, the main text, plate pages and all. (Next time you look to see how many pages a book has, check whether the preliminary pages have a separate sequence in Roman numerals, which can be useful from the publisher's point of view if the number of pages needed for the prelims is not known when the main text is paginated; and check whether any half-tone pages are included in the main sequence. For short books publishers often prefer to add all the page numbers together to produce the highest possible total.)

Although buyers are often unwilling to take them into account when assessing the value for money offered by a letterpress book, the photographs are the most costly ingredient. The copper or zinc blocks from which they are printed, the art paper, and the binding of the special plate pages combine to make these picture pages several times as expensive as the text ones. Their number must therefore be limited. If it appears that the subject cannot be covered satisfactorily without a very large number of photographs, the only solution may be to produce a 'picture book', with large pages printed on art paper throughout—or to run a picture book in parallel with the volume of text, which might then have only a few illustrations.

Line illustrations that can be printed on the text pages are a much easier proposition, at least providing there is no expensive drawing work involved. The necessary blocks are cheaper to make and can be printed at no greater cost than type on the ordinary text pages. And the use of these extra pages of ordinary, bulkier paper will make the book bigger and better value. Added to all that, they are still illustrations! So publishers who have to be mean in the allocation of plate pages are often generous in accommodating line drawings. The only line work that a publisher avoids wherever he can is folding maps and plans. These have to be printed separately and often folded, as well as tipped-in to the book, by expensive hand labour. They give poor value for money and again tend not to be taken into account by buyers assessing a book's value. Usually it will be cheaper to have three or four separate line illustrations on the pages of a book, each perhaps going across two pages, than a single folding plan. Printing a map on the book pages of course limits its size, but judicious use can be made of double-page spreads in the middle of 16-page sections. Ideally maps for double-page spreads need drawing with as little detail down the middle as possible; some material tends to disappear in the central gutter.

Details of the kinds of pictures that can be used as line illustrations on text pages, and those that must be reproduced as half-tones on plate pages, are given in chapter 5.

Colour pictures should also be mentioned. Lithography and gravure enable popular books with substantial print runs to carry many colour pictures, often at comparatively low published prices—especially low if an international 'hook-up' between publishers has been possible and the pictures for books whose texts may later be printed in various languages are all machined in one operation. But for a letterpress book with a first print order in the 2,500-5,000 range, colour is a much less practical proposition. Full colour may cost up to £100 a page, or roughly what twenty text pages would cost. And again, though of course they like colour pictures, most book buyers regard them as optional extras, nice decorations which should not be reflected in an increased published price.

The only place where colour is often commercially justified is on the jacket. Having made a colour-block set for the jacket, many publishers are willing to use it a second time to provide a frontispiece—the identical picture, but in a less damageable position, often better produced than on the jacket, on real art paper and given a caption. To secure maximum economy, some publishers print the colour blocks from a number of book jackets all together on the same sheet of art paper which is then split up to form the frontispieces for the various books—perhaps each of them otherwise printed by a different printer. To justify further colour blocks in a semi-specialist or specialist non-fiction book printed by letterpress is often difficult. Even if another three pages of colour are added, at a cost that must be reflected in the published price, they still scarcely make a splash. The few colour pictures may indeed merely emphasise the lack of colour in the majority of the book, spoiling the impact of excellent black-and-white photographs.

BINDING AND JACKET

Binding is normally the aspect of a book's production that least affects the author, except that during the age the binding process seems to take he may feel that everyone has forgotten his baby. In fact few people in Britain have strong views on binding details for the types of books considered here, simply expecting them to be conventional and workmanlike.

This brings us back to the point made earlier. New non-fiction books are conventionally hardbacks; their fairly high price is not because the hardback binding is particularly expensive but because this is the way publishers recoup their initial outlay on the whole production and editorial process, and arrange for authors to be fairly rewarded. Conversely, paperback binding is not especially cheap until very large quantities of the same title are involved. The popular paperback is what is known as 'perfect' bound: each page is a separate entity instead of being part of a folded sheet, and is held in place by glue applied under pressure and heat. But today there are many intermediate stages between the true hardback and the perfect-bound paperback; when, for instance, non-fiction books of a semi-specialist nature are issued in a cheaper edition they are often given stout paper covers with the same quality paper and the same sewing of the pages and sections as in the hard-back edition.

To repeat the point that perplexes so many authors and

bookbuyers, it does not follow that these paper-covered editions are much cheaper to produce than the hardback ones, and it would in fact probably be cheaper to bind the entire print order in one format, rather than two; publishers produce the two versions simply because while libraries and many individuals will want the more expensive, hardback one, an additional and quite separate market among students and others can be tapped at the lower price. Even where the paperback form is expensive as paperbacks go, with a price of say half that of the bound edition, many publishers of course leave a gap between putting the two editions on the market so that the keenest buyers take the more expensive version, yielding the greatest proportionate as well as actual return to publisher and author.

In Britain few buyers notice if the publisher of a hardback book spends extra money on real instead of imitation cloth, or on more or better gold blocking. American standards are higher, and a book produced in Britain for sale on both sides of the Atlantic is given a better binding for its special American than its ordinary home edition. It used to be said that the Americans were fussier about their bindings because unless a heavier board were used the binding cases would warp in centrally-heated houses. In fact the stricter requirements go beyond that; most American publishers who import special editions of British-produced books also demand real cloth.

The jacket is the last, but still a vitally important, part of the physical book. Many authors are surprised to learn that it is the first part to be produced by some publishing houses. Its early emergence is for publicity purposes: the publisher's representatives solicit orders from booksellers by showing it, and public-library suppliers circulate their customers with advance copies.

Originally the jacket, a fairly modern innovation in the history of books, was genuinely a 'dustcover' designed merely to protect. Today its publicity and sales function is far more important than its protective one, though it must still be stout enough not to be torn on booksellers' shelves. With, probably, an illustration which must be chosen with great care and which might be informative as well as eye-catching, with its blurb describing the book's basic aims and achievements, with perhaps a note about the author and a description of some of the same publisher's other books, the jacket can be almost a miniature magazine and is certainly costly to produce, perhaps accounting for a tenth of a book's total budget.

Authors are often asked to provide or suggest illustrations suitable for use on the jacket and to write a rough blurb.

Considerable experience is needed actually to design a successful jacket; indeed, talk about jackets accounts for much conversation among publishers and their sales representatives. A good jacket, attractive, compelling, but above all giving the right indication of the book's character, produced and circulated punctually (which may mean three months ahead of publication) can take the book halfway to success, while many an excellent work has been killed by a bad or just unsuitable jacket.

Increasingly public libraries find jackets so useful, attractive and informative that they fix them permanently in position around the book, even if the book has been rebound to give it extra strength for library use. Since the jacket's flaps wrap round the inside of the binding case, they obliterate part of any endpaper map or decoration the book may have. Covering up a decoration does not matter unduly, but blotting out part of a map or diagram essential to the understanding of the book certainly does. Endpaper maps have long been unpopular with libraries, but today more than ever should be avoided—unless the map can be repeated within the book where it will not be partly obliterated.

4   Your Manuscript

MAKE IT EASY TO READ AND HANDLE

HOWEVER MUCH a publisher may love books (and most of them are in the book business because they do), he rarely enjoys handling the actual manuscript. At best it will be taken for granted, the presentation not impeding the absorption of the words. At worst it will cause infinite frustration, making intelligent reading nigh impossible; the reader may even start by cutting a finger with some gruesome metal fastening in one of those ferociously complicated binders that inexperienced authors occasionally seek out.

A typewritten page starts by being larger than the page of a conventional book, and any extra encumbrance such as an elaborate binder adds unnecessarily to size and weight. Manuscripts have to be posted between staff, carried home in briefcases, read late in the evenings and even in bed, consulted in cars and on trains: keep their sheer physical bulk to the minimum. Avoid the elaborate binder that may be useful for storing work intended to be consulted only occasionally. Ring binders are especially unpopular since the publisher cannot easily discard them—or if he does take the manuscript pages off the ring, they may take a considerable time to thread back neatly. A petty enough objection—but to someone working under pressure and handling pieces of manuscript all day, a battle with the mechanics can be the last straw. Speaking personally, I like a loose manuscript without any kind of binding or fastening except for big paperclips holding together the pages of each individual chapter. The ideal container is nothing more elaborate than the box in which the typing paper was bought, or failing that a shirt box or something similar.

At present most publishers and printers prefer quarto sheets (10 by 8 inches) but new international sizes may soon become popular. Larger sizes such as foolscap should be avoided, since they are less convenient to handle, whether they are being read by the publisher in bed on Sunday morning or set by the printer on a monotype machine (where the foolscap sheet usually has to be folded in two while the quarto one can be visible all at one time). Certainly keep to the same-sized paper and typing throughout, and always type in full double spacing, leaving ample margins at top and bottom and a clear one and a half inches down the left. The more even the typing and margins, the easier it will be to 'cast off' the manuscript (estimate its length).

A reasonable number of clear handwritten corrections or crossings-out do not matter. Your manuscript should not seek to be a prize exhibit for a village show, but merely to be businesslike and clear in all its details. If you must make more changes than can be comfortably accommodated between the typed lines or in the margins, retype a portion and paste it over the appropriate part of the original. If the new version is longer than the old, or whenever substantial additional material has to be injected midway down a page, the original sheet should be cut right across, the new matter being pasted or sellotaped on to it in the correct position; any lines displaced at the bottom of the original sheet should then be pasted to a fresh sheet of the same size; however few lines of copy this holds it should then be numbered into the sequence. This system ensures that the printer is presented with material in the right order on pages all of the same size, and is not expected to take in copy on a second sheet while he is midway down the first sheet—a time-wasting process, with the risk that the operator will forget to go back and complete the first page. Never stick or staple small pieces of paper to the edge of the manuscript.

The manuscript pages should of course be numbered consecutively throughout. I say 'of course', but many authors still present their work without any page numbers whatsoever, or with the numbers beginning afresh at 1 for each chapter. Consecutive numbering throughout is not mere ritual: it enables the publisher to make an intelligent guess at the book's overall number of words without having to count the pages individually or add up the numbers of pages in the individual chapters; and enables him confidently to detach pages from the manuscript for closer study, perhaps to compare the contents of one section with another, without the nightmare possibility of creating an unsortable muddle. If additional sheets are added after the numbering has been done, they should carry the same numbers as the previous sheets plus a, b, c etc. If one of the original sheets ceases to exist after deletions have been made, indicate 'no number 32' or mark page 31 '31-2' so that printer or publisher quickly sees what has happened.

A table of contents with the manuscript-page numbers marked in pencil can usefully help the publisher or his reader find his way round; but do not type in the numbers, since obviously they will not correspond with the ultimate printed-page numbers. Similarly, within your text it can help to add in pencil the numbers of manuscript pages referred to, while typing XX to indicate to the printer that the correct printed page number will be supplied in proof.

The top copy of the manuscript should be on good-quality typing paper that will stand fair wear and tear. At least one carbon or photo copy and preferably two should be taken, using flimsier paper. One of the copies should be retained by the author for safety's sake in case of loss in the post or fire in the publisher's office; but the publisher may also request a copy, or be pleased to receive one without requesting it, so that he can get the book estimated by a printer while the top copy is being sub-edited, and later can have a copy by him in the office when the top manuscript is with the printer or perhaps send one to an American publisher who may buy a special edition.

All corrections and changes, including changes in pagination, should be carefully made on all copies so that they exactly tally. Many a muddle could have been avoided had the author taken the trouble to renumber the carbon copy he retained when renumbering the top copy despatched to the publisher.

The publisher will give basic instructions to the printer, but an author can help by indicating, for instance, any special deviations from the standard house style and any possible elasticity in the placing of tables, or the layout of awkward quotations. Directions to the printer should ideally be written in a different coloured ink or begin with a bold PRINTER so that the comment does not look like part of the manuscript itself. As will be seen in the next chapter, the position of line illustrations should also be boldly marked in the margins.

THE FINAL PREPARATION

For reasons of economy (in time as well as money) more and more books go straight into page proofs, avoiding those tedious galleys. This short cut benefits both author and publisher if all goes smoothly, which means if everything was sent to the printer in its correct and final form. But any extensive revisions, especially any changes in the order of the material, are more expensive to make on page proofs than on galleys, and will necessitate a second set of proofs to check the corrections.

So the manuscript should be finished off as though it were in fact the first proof. If it is so untidy that you cannot trust your own checking, retype the troublesome pages. The cost of retyping will be negligible compared with that of making changes once the work is set up in type. If a situation described in your book is changing rapidly, emphasise the difficulty to your publisher and try to arrange to have the manuscript back to make essential last-minute changes just before it gets committed to type. If the proofs then follow within a couple of months, few further changes should be needed.

Mark clearly where all 'extract' matter such as quotations and tables is to go, whether quotations are to be indented and put in smaller type, where line illustrations are to be placed and with what captions, and decide on your system of headings and subheading. Even the injection of an extra heading, or just an increase in the weight and size of an existing heading, may be enough to render the proofed page too long, resulting in the expensive and irritating business of the last line(s) having to be taken to the top of the following page, perhaps setting up a chain reaction throughout the rest of the chapter. Insertion of a footnote can do the same. If you prepare your final manuscript meticulously you will fail to understand why some other authors find proof-reading such a headache. And your publisher will love you.

With proper organisation and foresight, almost any book, even those including a fair number of line illustrations to go in the text, can be proofed straight into page form if there is only a single column of text on the page. Galley proofs cannot, however, be omitted for the more complicated kinds of layout, especially if there are two or more columns per page; in those cases the publisher may indeed find it necessary to paste up a layout using galley proofs of the text and block pulls of illustrations.

Although you will have marked on the manuscript the positions for all drawings, maps and diagrams to appear on the text pages, do not include the illustrations themselves; these should be placed in a separate folder, with their captions and with a clear numbering sequence of their own and cross-referencing to the manuscript page-numbers concerned. Photographs and their captions should be placed in another separate folder (see chapter 5).

HEADINGS AND NOTES

Chapter headings should be clearly indicated at the beginning of each chapter of the manuscript, and so far as the subject allows should be of roughly the same length for all chapters in the book. It helps to make them reasonably short since they are normally used as the running head at the top of the right-hand pages.

Decide whether or not you need subheadings and work out a consistent scheme which can be applied to the book as a whole. The actual typography or layout will be decided by the publisher, but make clear the relative 'weight' or importance of each heading. For instance, the main chapter title can be typed in upper and lower case (small letters except for a capital initial letter for important words); the main section headings should then be centred in block capitals; a third category of heading, to mark divisions within the material covered by the main section or subheading, could then be placed at the side in upper and lower case and underlined to appear in italics. In addition, you can indicate the relative weight by placing a letter beside the headings—A for the full chapter heading, B for the main section or subheading, C for the side heading, and even D if yet another division is necessary. Lack of clarity and consistency can cause untold confusion, not only to the publisher, editor and printer, but (if they do not correct matters) to the book's readers.

Notes and references must also be treated consistently. What notes are needed and why? Differentiate in your mind between the note that elaborates on a particular point or gives additional information, and the reference which merely quotes the source of information. Both kinds may be placed at the foot of the page, or both kinds consolidated at the end of the book, or you can rationally place a relatively small number of genuine notes at the foot of the page while having the source references at the back of the book. If the notes are to appear at the foot of the page, type them immediately after the line to which they refer, but rule them off from the ordinary text. If they are to appear at the end of the book, of course type them in sequence on separate sheets.

Where notes are consolidated at the end of the book (the cheaper and often the tidier method), they are normally numbered from 1 up consecutively, starting a new sequence for each chapter. Raised index numbers are inserted on the text page in the relevant positions, preferably at the end of a sentence. Any footnotes appearing actually on the text pages are normally indicated by symbols: the first by an asterisk *, the second by a dagger †. A single note at the foot of the last page of each chapter can indicate the page number (to be completed in proof) on which that chapter's notes will be found; and in the notes section at the back you can quote the number and title of each chapter and indicate which text pages it occupies. This simple cross-referencing largely overcomes the objection that notes at the back of the book are inconvenient to use. Remember that there is a two-way traffic between text and notes, for some people may read the notes for their own interest and want to refer readily back to the text.

If, on the other hand, all notes are to appear at the foot of the pages, they are usually numbered, starting at 1 for each page. Never number notes consecutively throughout a complete book, since should there be a single addition or deletion in sub-editing or for any other reason, all those that follow will need changing.

Even in the academic book it is often possible to avoid notes altogether by making simple explanations or citing sources in brackets; (Smith, David, 1969) adequately refers the reader to the full entry in the bibliography (*Industrial Britain: The North West*, 1969). Simply to explain 'As David Smith has said' is perhaps the most readable approach when your book is intended partly for readers unused to the conventions of academic books.

The way in which book titles, and titles of journals and articles, should be printed in notes and citations as well as in the bibliography is stated in the note on bibliographies in the END PAGES section of this chapter. Where full details of a book, journal or other material are given in the bibliography, an abbreviated version is adequate for the notes; and when a particular source is cited repeatedly, again use an abbreviated version for each reference after the first. This is more helpful to the reader than to use the old-fashioned 'op cit' or 'ibid'.

HOUSE STYLE

Authors should also seek consistency in smaller details such as the capitalisation and spelling of words, punctuation and the use of abbreviations.

Most publishers have their own 'house' or 'preferred' style booklets, issued in printed or duplicated form to authors and their typists. Some publishers rely on the famous *Hart's Rules* to give guidance; originally the rules were developed and printed solely for the guidance of Oxford University Press authors, staff and printers, but they have been far more widely adopted, though many firms now use a simpler, more modern style. Some firms also use *Collins' Authors' and Printers' Dictionary*. When writing a commissioned work, or a book which it is hoped a particular publisher will accept, it is obviously sensible to adopt that house's chosen style, with single or double quotation marks, a stop or no stop after abbreviations like Mr and ft, and so on.

Where no particular publisher is in mind, all that matters is that the style is uniform—that if single quotation marks are used on the first page they are used consistently throughout (quotations within quotations being in double quote marks), that feet and inches are not spelt out in full on one line, abbreviated as ft and ins on the next and as ft. and in. on the third. Stick to nationalisation or nationalization, the Chairman or the chairman (where there is doubt normally the capital is dropped these days), m.p.h., mph or miles per hour. Where you are employing a typist (or asking your wife) to prepare the final manuscript, make sure that she knows what is wanted.

Few publishers expect perfection, though all appreciate finding it. What is needed is a reasonable degree of help to cut down the amount of changes the sub-editor has to make to the manuscript before it goes to the printer. The fewer the ink marks, the clearer the manuscript will be, the greater the chance the sub-editor has of spotting any more serious inconsistencies, the less the chance of the printer making mistakes.

On at least one occasion I have positively been swayed into accepting a manuscript whose content had some shortcomings because it was beautifully typed and consistently presented in our house style, chapter headings, note arrangements and all. By following our style the author made it plain that he had studied our method and designed the book for us, and the work he saved us in correcting house style partly covered (and certainly sweetened!) the extra editorial costs we incurred in strengthening the basic text.

PRELIMINARY PAGES

A careful author supplies copy for the preliminary pages, or 'prelims', and for the end pages. Each page should be typed on a separate sheet of paper. The prelims are normally made up as follows.

Half-title page   This merely carries the book's main title, typed on an otherwise blank sheet of copy paper.

Half title verso   The page at the back of the half-title is sometimes left blank, but if the author wants to list his previous books he should do so on the sheet representing this page. If the book is appearing in a series, the publisher may wish to list the other volumes instead or additionally.

Title page   The author can set out the title, sub-title if any, his name and any degrees or qualifications he thinks relevant enough to display. If the book has been commissioned he can even add the publisher's name.

Title verso   The page at the back of the title contains the copyright notice (which the author may be able to sketch out after seeing what is done in other books), the Standard Book Number (which only the publisher can supply) and a statement of where the book was printed, for which publisher at what address (again, the publisher will supply).

Dedication   If there is to be a dedication or quotation, this should follow next. The publisher should have it at the start so that he can provide for it when the manuscript is cast off. Especially if to save pages would help to produce an even printing working, a short dedication or quotation is sometimes accommodated on the title verso. If however it is given the prominence of the right-hand page opposite the title verso, then the page that follows it (normally the sixth text page in the book) will be blank.

Table of contents   The author can set this out by following the style adopted by a table of contents in a book of a similar kind. If chapters are broken into sections with sub-headings, each subheading may be listed under the chapter title as is done in this book. As hinted earlier, it helps the publisher find his way around a manuscript if the manuscript-page numbers can be inserted in pencil, the final printed-page numbers of course having to wait until the book is in page proof.

List of illustrations   Again the author can provide it, by following the style of the list in a similar book. Fairly abbreviated captions are given here, though sometimes the list also acknowledges the sources of the illustrations. Half-tones are usually listed first and then line illustrations in a second sequence under a sub-heading 'IN THE TEXT'; this is partly because until the book is in page proof you cannot tell where the half-tones and illustrations will fall in relation to each other, making it impossible to provide in advance a single list of all types of illustration in the correct sequence.

Preface/Foreword   This is an optional extra less frequently used than in the past. Today people increasingly like to judge a book themselves on its own merit, and a preface either by the author or by some famous personage he has persuaded to help 'sell' the work cuts less ice—or can even arouse a hostile reaction. A simple explanation of how the book came to be written and its aims can sometimes be useful, and the author

E

can also use the preface or foreword to thank those who have given him help en route. Very rarely is both a preface and a foreword needed in a book of ordinary length and scholarship.

Introduction If personal acknowledgments are not included and the introduction is an integral part of the book, introducing the subject matter rather than the book itself, this can be numbered as the first chapter; otherwise it is usually outside the chapter sequence.

For books of the kind discussed here many publishers prefer to cut the introductory fuss to the minimum, getting straight into objective matter, and concentrating both personal comments and thanks by the author less conspicuously at the end of the book. I personally feel this way for two reasons: the reader does not generally want to begin by wading through personal details, including thanks to the author's wife for her tact and endurance while the book was being written; and too many authors (especially those of some academic prestige, anxious above everything to avoid false claims for their work) start a preface or introduction by listing all the faults and omissions, leaving the potential reader with the impression that the work must be a marginal exercise of little solid merit.

END PAGES

Where all or any of the following are to be included, they are placed at the end of the book. The following is the usual order though there is no hard-and-fast rule.

Gazetteer A gazetteer or an amplified geographical list of any kind, supplied as a basic part of the book as distinct from an appendix, is useful when dealing with certain kinds of subjects (such as archaeology) and is normally placed before the end-matter proper.

Postscript This can be a useful extra in which, for instance, the author can make forecasts or express personal views in a manner not acceptable within the basic chapter framework of a factual book.

Notes and references   If notes are necessary and are not carried at the foot of each individual page, they normally appear immediately after the close of the continuous text. The notes for each chapter should be presented separately under a sub-heading carrying that chapter's number, title and preferably also text-page numbers to facilitate cross-reference between notes and text.

Appendices   As the word implies, these are extras not essential to the understanding of the basic book, and therefore they usually come after the notes documenting or amplifying the chapters. An appendix may provide additional material, such as the complete text of an historic document, a note on research methods, or an example of how things are organised in a different country; or it can repeat information given in the text in a different, often statistical, form. Thus while the text may have dealt with salient points about the dividend record in a company history, an appendix might list the complete dividend performance from the start. Good appendices can give a book an additional dimension, but if the material is thin and suspect it will look even more bogus standing on its own here than incorporated into a chapter. Statistical matter must not of course require more columns than can comfortably be accommodated on the text page or a pair of facing text pages. Publishers are even less likely to agree to folding tables of statistics than to folding maps, since it is usually possible to break down statistical matter into smaller tables, more easily manageable and more comprehensible.

Bibliography   Any good non-fiction book needs a bibliography, both to tell the reader where the author found his information and as a signpost to further reading and research material. Indeed, if you have to make a quick judgment on a book, the bibliography is as revealing as any part, and its quality is often mentioned in reviews in learned journals. Bad bibliographies are not only incomplete but lack a rational plan and give inadequate or varying information about the books and other sources listed.

The best plan is to list general works first and then to categorise more specialist works, though sometimes it is easier to list books and other sources individually for each chapter. Guidance about which books and sources proved particularly useful to the author (and might therefore help the reader who wants further information) should be given wherever possible: a list including every conceivable publication on a subject without any hint about its nature or usefulness is usually a waste of space—and certainly do not blindly include references to publications you have not consulted yourself. Perhaps the most useful bibliographies are those with discursive introductions that comment on the main works consulted before printing a formal list. In the formal list, within each category or chapter section, the order of presentation must be consistently alphabetical by author or chronological by original date of publication (preferably the first).

Distinguish carefully between the titles of books and of chapters in books or articles in journals. Titles of books and of journals should be underlined to appear in italics, while the names of chapters and of articles within these books and journals go in quotation marks and not italics since they are not publications in their own right:

> BOOKER, FRANK. *The Industrial Archaeology of the Tamar Valley*. David & Charles, Newton Abbot, 1967.
>
> BOOKER, FRANK. 'The Tamar Valley', *Industrial Archaeology*, 1967.

In a book of academic standing the publishers' names should consistently be quoted. In Britain the convention is to mention the publisher's town only if it is not London. Make sure that you refer to the last edition of the books listed.

Acknowledgments and author's notes My own firm encourages authors to consolidate these in one section at the end of the book, after the bibliography, but practice varies. Certainly acknowledgments must be made to all those who have given substantial help (including perhaps the cartographer), but do not give more offence than pleasure by misspelling names or quoting names in a shorter version (perhaps with only initials) than authors and others 'trade' under in public life. If Dr A. Jones has secured a university chair, change him to Professor A. Jones. Illustration sources must all be acknowledged here or elsewhere; authors who promise to acknowledge the use of a picture and then fail to do so cause their publishers if not themselves much embarrassment.

Index This is the author's responsibility and no one who has written a book to be useful, as distinct from just making money, will lack interest in its quality. It may be necessary to employ someone else (the publisher may find someone on the author's behalf) to do the actual labour of collating the entries and placing them in alphabetical order, but even then the author should give the necessary starting guidance and exercise quality control.

A few books may need two or more indexes, but where possible consolidate all entries into a single sequence. The best indexes are not necessarily the longest and certainly not the most complicated; the aim should be to include all topics *of importance*, making the best use of the space available if this is limited, and on a scale suited to the book concerned. Especially in shortish books whose prices have to be kept low and where the economy of an even printing working is essential, be prepared to make last-minute cuts to fit a smaller space if need be.

A brief note at the head of the index explaining its scope may be useful, and can indicate any particular system adopted, for instance that Acts of Parliament are listed under their individual titles, and that page numbers in bold type (indicated on the typescript by wavy underlining) refer to the principal entries or to illustrations as the case may be. If the book is within a series, then follow the general series scope of the index as well as its precise layout.

The index cannot of course be completed until the book is in page proof, but delay at that stage has to be kept to the minimum. So make the framework in advance, from a carbon copy of the manuscript; even if the publisher has asked for the only carbon copy at the start of production, he may be able to return it for index use long before the proofs are due. The most thorough approach is probably to underline on the manuscript all the items you want indexed, and then to build up a card-index system, typing from the cards once they have been checked and arranged in alphabetical order.

Type in double or treble spacing, with wide margins, so that any last-minute changes can be made without loss of legibility—and take at least one carbon. Make abundantly plain which are the main entries, and which are sub-headings under a main one. Use the same styles as elsewhere in the book, though for an index some abbreviations may be necessary; use these consistently. Accurate punctuation is vitally important in an index: normally a comma (or occasionally a colon) is used after the item you are indexing, with a comma after each page number and a semi-colon at the end of each sequence within a composite entry.

Where the book concentrates on one main theme, such as the history of merchant shipping, the life of a statesman, or a particular breed of dog, it is usually sensible to omit any general entry for that subject. A long string of sub-headings is difficult to use, and in any case the reader is likely to look for an entry for the particular aspect he wants. All other important topics must have entries, and where a long string of page numbers accumulates these entries should be subdivided. In the following example, the page numbers immediately following the main heading are indexing the references to Italy as a whole and in general; the subheadings pick out the references to individual aspects. It helps to arrange the subheadings in alphabetical order.

Italy, 37, 73, 111–13; agriculture, 36–7, 146; architecture, 153–5; history, 2–13, 150–1, 200; industries, 30, 99, 203–10; transport 95–7, 213–15.

When a subject is dealt with more or less continuously on several successive pages, specify the first and last of the sequence: 125–8. When, however, there are only slight and unconnected references, list the page numbers separately (125, 126, 127, 128) or state 125ff.

Cross-referencing is useful when tackled with moderation. Where only a few page numbers are concerned, it is better to repeat them under two headings than to send the reader from one entry to another with a *'see'* reference; but where a composite entry with various subheadings is involved, and the reader may not be sure where to look, then help: Pottery, *see* Porcelain; Occupations, *see* Employment. *See also* references at the end of an entry can help establish connections between different subjects, and in particular can be used to send the reader from a general to a particular entry: Metals, 68–9, 114: *see also* Gold (or: *see also* under individual metals).

When the subject is mentioned in a footnote, add *n* to the page number. Illustrations, too, should be indexed, their page numbers appearing at the end of the sequence for the subject concerned and being underlined to denote italic or bold type.

5   The Illustrations

THEIR IMPORTANCE

ILLUSTRATIONS ARE an important ingredient of most non-fiction books and from the production point of view are often the main feature that distinguishes them from novels and makes them more costly. The interest of booksellers, the number of individuals who buy on impulse, the size of the carefully-scrutinised orders from institutions working to tight budgets and the quality of reviews in the press may all substantially depend upon the success with which the author has been able to match his words with his illustrations. Reviewers of non-fiction will often praise the basic text but censure the quality of the maps, or the lack of imagination in the choice of photographs or the poorness of their reproduction.

Most publishers regard illustrations as being basically the responsibility of the author. Not only does the inclusion of the illustration increase the price of the finished book on which the author's royalties are calculated, but the author should be the best judge of how to illustrate his subject and should normally know where the best material is to be found. The publisher should help with both general and technical advice, and sometimes may be able to give specific assistance in finding a particular picture, but the prime responsibility rests with the author. Of course there are well-known authors who refuse pointblank to have anything to do with illustrations, failing to see their potential in strengthening the book as a whole or perhaps knowing that anything they write will sell well enough with minimum attention from them; their publishers may be so pleased to have their books that they accept the position. This book, however, is addressed to the less established writer who may not be able to dictate terms and who in any case will be anxious to build up his subject or his own reputation. Indeed, it is easier for the publisher to undertake the selection of pictures for wide-ranging popular books covering obvious subjects than for the more specialist works with which we are mainly concerned here.

The maximum possible enthusiasm should be brought to the task of finding illustrations. The best collections of photographs are those that have been *selected* from larger collections. Do not examine just enough pictures to fill the space; do not begrudge having to leave out some subject in the final selection, especially if better ones turn up. The discovery of two unpublished historic photographs at the last minute may make all the difference to the interest of the illustrations in the assessment of many readers. Readers are not slow to discover where authors have taken the easiest course, or indeed to discover the weaknesses in a poor map. Conversely, everyone appreciates pictures that not only look good but genuinely complement the text and are well cross-referenced with it.

The biggest mistake is to forget all about illustrations until the writing of the book has been completed. The best selection can probably not be assembled in a hurry: picture agencies, museums and individual photographers often take a considerable time to reply to enquiries, and half a dozen different leads may have to be followed before success is achieved. As soon as you have decided to write a book on a certain subject, open a file for pictures or facts about the whereabouts of known pictures, and initiate enquiries at the earliest opportunity. The final page-by-page arrangement may be best left till the text has been finished, but then it will be too late, for instance, to write a letter for publication in local newspapers asking owners of interesting old photographs on a particular district or subject to let you borrow them for your forthcoming work—often a very productive means of discovering pictures that have not been published before.

As we have seen, from the production point of view there

are two main types of illustrations: line illustrations and photographs or half-tones.

LINE ILLUSTRATIONS

Unless art paper is used for the whole book, the line illustrations are normally placed on the text pages, and if the book is to be set straight into page proofs they will be needed by the publisher and the printer simultaneously with the manuscript. They should not however be interleaved with the manuscript but should be sent in a separate folder or envelope since they will first have to go to the blockmaker, even if they do not need redrawing.

As stated earlier, the line illustrations and the manuscript must be cross-referenced so that the illustrations will be placed correctly in position. Each line illustration should be allotted a number which should be indicated clearly at the appropriate point in the manuscript (preferably in coloured ink or crayon to stand out boldly), while the manuscript-page number should also be marked on the illustration. This double check is valuable, since line-illustration material is apt to come in varying shapes and sizes and sometimes has to be packed in more than one container, for instance envelopes despatched with the manuscript and a roll for larger maps.

Remember that your manuscript and illustrations will not be the only ones arriving in the publisher's office by that post, and the editor concerned will probably not unpack them himself. Every package should be labelled with the book's title. Make clear how many line illustrations you are posting, with details of any that are to follow. (So far as possible keep them together.) For safety, perhaps ask the publisher to acknowledge receipt of the number of illustrations sent.

It sounds elementary, possibly, but mislaid line illustrations produce more than their fair share of nightmares in publishing offices. A precious original was once destroyed when an author sent my own firm several packages without any numbering system or any indication of how many items there should be in total. All were unpacked with ordinary care, and several items removed from within a roll, but who having emptied a roll would also look *between* the sheets of brown paper around the outside of it? Conversely, we have also had panic searches among wrapping paper for illustrations we thought would be coming only to discover on enquiry that the author did not send those particular ones with the rest.

Line illustrations normally fall into two kinds: original source material such as old handbills, engravings and extracts from letters, which will go straight to the blockmaker for reproduction; and maps, charts and diagrams which have to be especially drawn or redrawn.

With material already existing, once an illustration is selected as useful for the book concerned, the main considerations are whether it is in fact suitable for the line reproduction process and whether it will reduce satisfactorily in size for accommodation on the book's page.

Line illustrations are, as the term suggests, reproduced entirely by a series of lines. The image is either reproduced in black, or it is not reproduced at all. There is no gradation of tone, as there is in half-tone photographic reproduction, so the line originals must be in sharp black if they are to come out clearly. Old notices were often badly printed and can consist of gradations of greys and actual gaps where no ink was transferred from the type to the page, and therefore they may reproduce patchily, though they can sometimes be touched up before blockmaking. Fine hatching or pencil shading may not come out clearly. Old letters normally reproduce well; material from photocopying machines often does not, because it lacks a sharp, clear image, the grey of the printed or written matter sometimes coming out relatively little bolder than the greyish background of the surrounding areas. Send the publisher the original, rather than copied material, whenever possible; good line blocks can easily be made from line illustrations in other books, but of course remember copyright considerations. If you have to take copies, try and make them first-class photographs with the black a true black and no background blur. Remember also that if the material is very complicated, trouble may result when the size of the picture has to be reduced for your book: the white gaps between the black lines will 'fill in', resulting in a smudgy continuous black.

Turning to maps, charts and diagrams, the author may be able to provide only rough material—material that the publisher's draughtsman can follow to produce a professional result. Even if the author is only producing roughs, however, he should bear the page size and shape in mind, try to work to a correct scale (since it will be easier for the draughtsman or cartographer to do a straight copy than to establish the basic framework afresh), and make sure he includes everything he wants, with correct spelling (cartographers are human and painstaking, and imagine their reaction when told to change ten names and alter the location of a boundary on their neat maps because the author carelessly fed in the wrong information initially).

The demy octavo (8½ by 5½ inches) page can normally accommodate a map of 7½ by 5 inches, less any space that has to be left *underneath* the map for caption. A double-page spread can run to a width of 10 inches with a depth of 8 inches if there is no caption or the caption is fitted into the map area. Normally maps are drawn to a larger scale—often twice the size—than they are reproduced.

Some authors have the ability to produce finished maps ready for the blockmaker themselves, and if help can be given in this way the publisher will usually welcome this. Line blocks are not costly to make or to print, but professional drawing can be very expensive indeed, so any cost-saving assistance may mean the publisher will accept more maps than might otherwise be possible, or that he will be prepared to give some other concession. Even if the author cannot undertake mapwork himself, he may know a professional geographer, surveyor or someone else who can—and it especially helps if that person has knowledge of the subject matter. The result may well be more

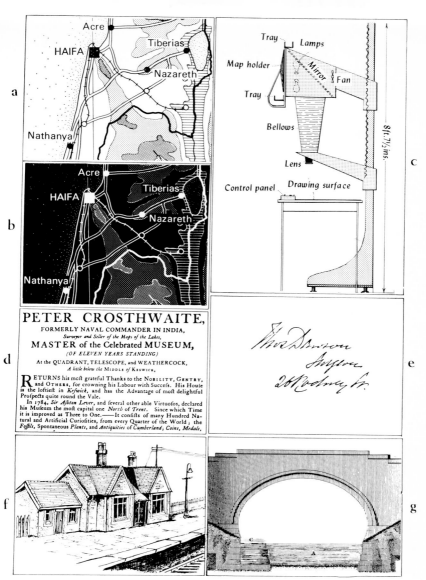

LINE SUBJECTS. Subjects to be reproduced as line blocks must consist entirely of solids, dots or lines with no intermediate grey tones. Tones are simulated by means of dot or line tints. **a** simple map in black ink on white incorporating dot and line tints **b** map incorporating the same detail as (a) but reversed to white on black **c** line drawing of equipment using self-adhesive tints to simulate tones **d** late eighteenth-century handbill **e** hand-writing from early nineteenth-century bookplate. Handwriting reproduces well in line providing that the ink is black and unfaded **f** line sketch with pen and indian ink **g** nineteenth-century engraving of canal bridge. The linework is dense black and the lines are sufficiently far apart to reproduce clearly on a line block. All subjects have been reduced by twice linear.

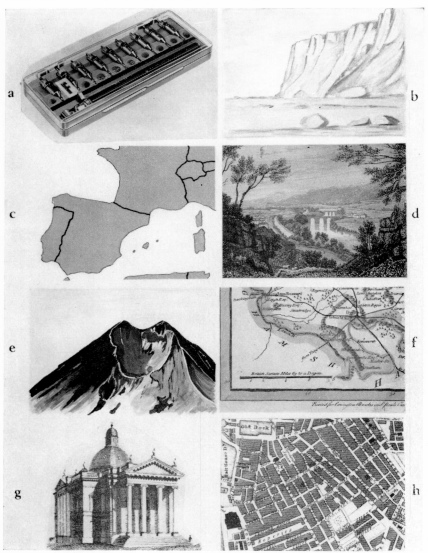

HALF-TONE SUBJECTS. The half-tone method is used to reproduce any subject which incorporates continuous tone. **a** photographic print of Standardgraph pens **b** pencil drawing with a soft pencil. The continuous tones of the pencil sketch reproduce softly and attractively by the half-tone process **c** map in which land areas are covered with solid grey tones (Zip-a-tone Medium Grey) which has to be broken down into a dot pattern by means of the half-tone screen **d** line engraving in which the lines are so fine and so closely spaced as to resemble continuous tone **e** wash drawing in diluted indian ink **f** early nineteenth-century hand-coloured map. The colour necessitates the use of the half-tone process—if the map were un-coloured a line block could have been made **g** & **h** these details from a nineteenth-century engraved map are doubtful subjects for the half-tone process. The building has reproduced nicely in this way but the half-tone screen has broken up the hatching on the map to produce an odd, striped pattern. These two subjects might have reproduced as well or even better by the line block method. All subjects have been reduced by twice linear.

purposeful as well as take a shorter time to produce—and if the work is done on a freelance basis and the fee can be paid direct to the cartographer, the cost will almost certainly be very much less than that to the publisher employing a salaried professional on his own staff. But if there is any doubt about your or your colleague's ability to provide the required quality, check carefully after a specimen map or two have been prepared. Often people who can draw good outlines spoil them by shaky or unsuitable lettering, or by unskilled use of stencils, while professional draughtsmen sometimes ignore the page size available.

These notes are only brief since for those seriously interested a companion volume, *Maps for Books and Theses*, by Alan Hodgkiss, the cartographer of the Department of Geography at the University of Liverpool, gives detailed advice with many dozens of actual examples of what to do, how to do it, and how to save time and gain accuracy by exploiting modern devices and techniques, and also covers aspects such as copyright.

HALF-TONES

Another companion volume, *Photography for Books and Reports*, by Brian Bracegirdle, deals with the technical considerations of taking photographs as well as the manner of presenting them, and again gives actual examples. Here I am concerned purely with salient points of selection and presentation, the approach being editorial rather than technical.

As was said earlier, while people expect many kinds of non-fiction books to be well illustrated, they are not normally prepared to pay a higher price for a double ration of pictures. Work realistically within the limitations laid down by the publisher—or the decision reached after bargaining with him. If you have only 16 pages of plates to cover a complicated subject, do not attempt to record everything you can by cramming in numerous small pictures on the page, ignoring all artistic considerations. Most readers do *not* expect to find a complete secondary documentation of the subject in picture form. They look instead for a well-balanced, representative selection, nicely presented, which usually means no more than two pictures to a page, perhaps 'bleeding' off the page's edge to make the fullest use of the art paper.

If there are 16 pages of plates, or even 24 in a longer book, it should be possible for the publisher to arrange for each page to appear opposite a page of text, in which case you can ask to have your captions placed at the foot of the text page, releasing the whole of the art paper for the pictures and perhaps enabling you to write longer captions. In these longer captions it may be possible to point out detail, which will to some extent compensate for the lack of separate pictures for every possible subject.

On the other hand if your subject is one which absolutely demands more pictures, maybe you should be producing a 'picture book' on art paper all through. What publishers cannot normally do is provide a full text and as many pictures as in a picture book all for the price of a conventional single volume. Unless the whole work is printed on art paper, your photographs will not usually appear opposite the text to which they refer, which is another reason why good captions (and cross-referencing) are required. But place the pictures so that the progression of subject matter is the same as that in the text, or adopt some other rational progression.

A paragraph of do nots! Do not give your publisher bad pictures of obvious subjects like the Forth Bridge, a bus or an animal which any competent photographer can take on any fine day; but a poorer standard is obviously acceptable in the truly historic and irreplaceable picture. Do not submit photographs of vehicles, machines or the like that just cut off outer limits such as the front of the front wheel or the top of a ship's rigging; if you cannot include the whole of the subject, cut part of it away boldly so that it does not look as though you hoped to include the lot and just failed. In a book that could appeal to a wider audience, do not concentrate entirely on close-ups of smaller details without any more general views or shots; the average reader will have less interest in minor details than you have.

Ideally the photographs should be full-plate or at least half-plate size, glossy prints with ample contrast. Pictures to be reproduced in black and white should be taken in black and white in the first place, since whatever satisfaction they may give for family purposes black-and-white prints off colour transparencies are often not good enough for blockmaking. Until there is a new technical breakthrough, specialist books are going to be illustrated mainly if not entirely in black and white. Yet today most people take colour pictures, and sometimes it is only when publication of a book approaches that it is suddenly realised that enough suitable negatives do not exist.

Label each photograph clearly on the back, and by all means indicate which part of the whole you would like reproduced if some of it is superfluous. Indeed, if say you have been allocated 16 pages of plates, why not produce a miniature 16-page layout showing by numbered rectangles on sheets of paper numbered 1 to 16 or whatever the total may be, roughly where each picture is to be placed? The very act of doing such a layout, however roughly, may make you change your choice, perhaps because you see it is not after all possible to place four essentially upright pictures on the same page, or maybe because you see a better way to obtain a rational progression between subjects. Let each picture for each page carry on the back the appropriate page number plus a, b, c, and then add the finishing helpful touch by placing all the photographs for each page in a separate, clearly-labelled envelope. NEVER stick photographs down in an album, or even use a postcard album from which it is difficult to remove and replace pictures speedily, since each picture may have to be handled individually several times during processing.

Though labelling of pictures is vitally important, never write on the photograph itself; marks made on the back can come through and appear on the blocks.

Only the reference number should appear on the back of the actual photographs, which the printer will never see. The captions list should be typed on separate sheets.

The same procedures can of course be adopted if the whole book is to be devoted to pictures. Publishers of picture books are pleased to let the author have layout sheets of the right size. Again, few authors will feel capable of doing the precise, finished layout, but basic guidance will help the publisher not only to keep the production costs down but to give the author as near as possible what he wants. The author will know what aspects will particularly interest certain classes of readers, where a large-scale reproduction of detail might be most helpful, and so on, whereas publishing staff not expert in the subject concerned are less likely to strike a right balance if left unaided to allocate space for perhaps 150 pictures.

Even in picture books the temptation to include a large number of small reproductions purely for record purposes should be resisted, for almost certainly most buyers and readers will demand generous treatment of the best topics, which may mean devoting whole pages and occasionally even double-page spreads to a single picture. And again, even in picture books try to produce a rational progression of material: the best result will probably be obtained by starting with a synopsis just as for any other book, allocating certain pages or sections to certain subjects.

PAYING FOR THE PICTURES

Most publishers expect their authors to clear the copyright of pictures, which may involve the payment of fees to agencies, museums and even colleagues in the profession or hobby. Sometimes publishers make a contribution toward the fees that authors have to pay.

Having to foot the bill will make the author budget-conscious, and certainly too much can be paid for permission to use pictures. But, if a publisher has provided a lump sum for picture copyrights, it is shortsighted to attempt to make a profit by retaining some of it: as we have said, the illustrations should be an integral part of a non-fiction book and its standing and sales may be affected by their quality. By all means argue with institutions about the size of their fees and seek reductions; but try to get the best.

Getting the best probably means not using exclusively your own pictures, but if you (or your wife or husband) can provide a proportion, so much the better. Writing a book is a lonely trail not only for the writer but for the partner not actively involved. If you are lucky enough to have a wife or husband who can handle the photographs, taking them him or herself or doing the research and dealing with agencies and museums, it turns the project into a team affair and also has useful tax advantages. But bad photographs or maps are still bad even if the work of your sweetheart; make sure she, or he, can do the job before embarrassing everyone, including the publisher.

£3 or more usually has to be paid to an institution or agency for the use of a single picture, but a reduction can often be negotiated if a dozen or more are chosen at the same time. If you pick a substantial number from the same source, ask if you can delay payment until the book's publication, when you may be receiving an advance from the publisher. Friends and colleagues are usually more modest in their financial demands and might be content with an acknowledgment and a free copy. But it will be your task, and not the publisher's, to provide the complimentary copy, and if it is to be an expensive book this may prove more costly than paying a fee.

In the United Kingdom photographs are protected by copyright for fifty years from *the end of the calendar year* after first publication, and copyright must of course be respected. But do not be put off using an interesting old picture if you genuinely cannot tell the date of original publication or trace the copyright owner; some postcards, for instance, could have been published equally well in 1915 or 1925, and their publishers have gone out of business. In such cases be prepared to

F

pay a fee should you be asked for one after your book has been published. Maps and artistic work normally enjoy copyright protection for fifty years after the artist's death. Special care should be taken to obtain permission for use of Ordnance Survey material, whether you want actually to reproduce part of an OS map or closely to adapt one for your own purposes. You do not avoid copyright liability by merely re-lettering or slightly amending someone else's basic work.

6 Your Publisher

THE CHOICE OF FIRM

PUBLISHERS' PERFORMANCES differ sharply. Some firms go for quick returns while others aim at long-term continuing sales. Some take little care with the physical production standards of their books while others always use the best materials and good designers. There are great differences in the approaches to aspects like publicity and the sales of subsidiary rights. One of the biggest contrasts is perhaps in the time that various firms take to convert a manuscript into a completed book.

In practice it is difficult to judge one firm's total performance against another's, to choose the publisher most suitable for your book in every respect, even if the perfect firm does in fact exist. The publishing scene is complex and firms are continually changing their character and their staffs; what would have been good guidance for particular kinds of books ten years ago might be irrelevant today. My own firm now has an annual output of nearly 200 books, but ten years ago was producing only half a dozen—to quote the nearest example at hand and remind the reader that since I am a publisher myself the advice in this chapter might be more biased than that in the rest of the book. But you can undertake some simple market research to avoid the worst pitfalls and waste of time. First, find out which publishers handle the kind of book you have written or plan to write. Unless you already know something about publishing, the best starting point will be the list of publishers in *The Writers' and Artists' Year Book*, which gives a brief description of the main types of book accepted. Unfortunately firms do not always keep their entries up to date, but at least make sure that you use the latest issue of the *Year Book*.

Send for the catalogues of likely-sounding firms and assess whether your book would look at home there (and check that the same firm has not already published a very similar kind of book too closely duplicating yours for the two to be viable under the same imprint). Go to your library or bookshop to see the books published by an individual publisher you have short-listed and compare them with books on the same subject issued by other publishers. Or subscribe to *The Times Literary Supplement* for a time and follow its many weekly columns of publishers' announcements. Study book reviews, especially in specialist magazines and learned journals covering your subject, noting the publishers and any praise or criticism of production standards and other aspects for which the publisher may have been directly responsible.

You need also to clarify your personal objectives. For instance, if your main aim is to produce a standard work that will enhance your prestige in your profession, the last thing you may want is a short period of high-pressure sales followed by the book being seen sold off cheaply on the bargain counters of bookstalls—so pick a publisher sympathetic to academic authors and one with a good record of keeping books alive through successive editions. Conversely, if your main interest is a quick financial return with a substantial advance against royalties, you will probably get it more easily from a large firm in a group than from a smaller, 'close' company.

Two of the points of greatest importance are unfortunately the hardest to check from outside. Many authors feel it is vital to know roughly how long a publisher will take to convert a manuscript into a finished book. While some firms seldom need more than twelve months or so, others habitually take two years and one can hear of a five-year gap between delivery of manuscript and publication. Then, the matter of subsidiary rights and export sales is more important than new authors may immediately realise, since the publisher really on the ball might be able to double or treble the income from ordinary royalties by selling translation, paperback, serialisation and other rights. On these two points especially it is useful to be able to consult another author who has been published by the firm you have in mind. If you cannot make enquiries on these points first, certainly you should raise them with the publisher once you have approached him and he has expressed an interest in your work.

An author cannot of course approach more than one firm at a time, and if the first publisher consulted expresses interest in publishing the manuscript much as it stands, but does not satisfy you in some respect, you take a gamble by turning to another. But presuming that your demands are reasonable, taking into account the sales potential of the manuscript concerned, the risk of doing so will not usually be great; if one house has offered to publish a book, the manuscript is presumably basically publishable, and though only a small proportion of the total manuscripts written ever reach the bookseller's shelves, there is no surplus of publishable work. Indeed there is a seller's market for many types of well-written non-fiction.

But the matter needs looking at in an entirely different light if a publisher accepts your work subject to your shortening, supplementing or changing it in some way, for that means that he does not regard it as publishable in its present form and others may not do so either. The first publisher you pick could be mad, but on the law of averages his advice, being born of experience, will be sound and it should be taken seriously. If you reject his plan to render the work publishable you may well find that some three months later you have to swallow very similar advice from another publisher who initially stood lower in your list of preferences. Publishers are not infallible, as is perhaps demonstrated by the rapid changes of staff and policies in many firms, but for the most part they are professionals and their basic assessments of treatment, length and scale of illustrations are apt to be uncannily similar—and right.

AGENTS

Publishers are used to having to bargain on royalties, on arrangements for subsidiary rights and on the time they will take in preparing a book for publication (as distinct from whether the book is basically publishable or not), if only because many authors engage agents to bargain on their behalf. Should you use an agent to find and negotiate with your publisher? There is no justification for the feeling among some authors that it is almost indecent to make a direct approach to a publisher; on the other hand a literary agent may be able to use his contacts and experiences to advantage on your behalf.

This is controversial ground, but on the whole agents come into their own more for the strictly literary type of book, including fiction and children's stories, than for definitive non-fiction. There are several reasons for this. More experience may perhaps be necessary in the proper placing of the strictly literary kind of book, while the exploitation of subsidiary rights is then often a very specialist operation which certainly the really successful novelist would not wish to get involved in himself. But for specialist or semi-specialist non-fiction, the choice of publisher may be quite easy, within the author's own powers to undertake, and possibly no more difficult than the choice of the literary agent. The choice of agent is indeed critical.

It may be the poorer variety of agency, struggling for existence, that makes the greatest display of pleasure at receiving an enquiry from you. Unfortunately there is no universally-accepted code of conduct, but the publishers of *The Writers' and Artists' Year Book* have made a point of listing only those agencies who are willing to complete a questionnaire and who undertake not to charge for advice—as distinct from claiming their commission on receipts resulting from their placing work. If you contemplate using an agency, stick to the list in the *latest* edition of *The Writers' and Artists' Year Book* and also read the editorial note at the head of the list.

Some of the larger and longer-established agencies have wide experience in handling non-fiction and are, for instance, as interested in long-term sales—their own 'backlist income'—as are good publishers. These more enlightened agencies will also encourage direct author-publisher contact on editorial or publicity points, providing of course they are left to handle all financial aspects.

At the other extreme there are some newer and smaller firms facing a short-term struggle to bring in enough cash. They are inevitably concerned to obtain the earliest and the biggest possible advances, regardless of long-term considerations. Sometimes an agent can genuinely and usefully obtain greater advances than individual authors less experienced in the ways of publishers; but advances are by no means everything, and make sure that your agent does not get his priorities and therefore even his choice of publisher wrong. Some less enlightened agencies also make it hard for author and publisher to develop ideas together by insisting that all correspondence be conducted through them.

Direct contact between author and publisher is often vitally important with non-fiction. As we have seen, the publisher frequently plays a major role in shaping the book's scope, approach or length. These works are not pure literature but attempt to do a positive job of work. They may justifiably be changed, or even contrived, to suit the requirements of a specific market, in a way that novels and more general books normally cannot be.

This is perhaps one reason why agents are less frequently used for non-fiction than for other types of book. Another reason is that subsidiary rights are usually less important. Handling translation, serial, paperback and bookclub rights for a successful novel can be a major undertaking requiring both time and skill. Even with non-fiction, the more likely a book is to have serial and translation possibilities, the more potentially useful it will be to have an agent.

Conversely, if there are no subsidiary rights prospects, and your book is only likely to earn £500 in royalties during the first three or four years, you cannot expect an agent to become very excited or do a great deal for you—unless of course he sees you as an author worth cultivating. Agents normally deduct 10 per cent of the gross royalties when paying their authors, so that the agent's share of £500 would be only £50, and that does not buy much time in a professional office these days. Many agents make their kill out of a small number of outstandingly successful authors and books, and these naturally obtain their best attention.

MAKING THE FIRST APPROACH

There is only one golden rule, and that is to remember that publishers judge their authors by their ability to *write*. The approach should be a written one. You may have the patience to wait until you have completed the entire manuscript, and submit this with, ideally, a short letter, a one or two-page outline of the book so that the publisher or his reader can immediately see the scope before becoming embroiled in the manuscript itself; also send return postage in case the work is rejected. But you may well prefer to have at least an expression of encouragement from a publisher before writing the whole book, and some publishers themselves like to comment at an earlier stage. So it may be sensible to send the letter and the outline or synopsis, possibly accompanied by a specimen chapter (not the introduction, which is usually untypical) to demonstrate your ability to put the plan into execution. If you have already published a book, or even a major contribution to a journal, of course tell the publisher and perhaps send a copy of that too.

But whatever you do, *write*. Do not at this stage call or telephone. Publishers must judge authors on their ability to communicate on paper, and even a short letter conveys some impression of that ability or lack of it. You will not, at least as yet, be judged for your ability to shine in a television interview. An important secondary reason for writing is that letters and synopses can be circulated among staff and outside advisers at the publisher's convenience. Meetings between publishers and authors are sometimes extremely fruitful, and often friendships develop, but let the publisher take the initiative. Even if you do not receive a reply to your first letter for some weeks and feel it necessary to chase him, do so in writing. Do not be like the author who once telephoned me to say that he would have to accompany his manuscript since he was doubtful if it would mean much unless he was there to explain it!

All this may seem obvious, but one of the biggest trials in the publisher's life is the number of people—including friends, and friends of friends, and the friends of friends of your most distant relations—who hope to gain some initial advantage by making personal contact. 'You cannot trust the post these days,' is the commonest argument used for seeking an appointment. 'I had better come with it myself.' If you really cannot trust the post, deliver the parcel to the publisher's door *anonymously*.

There are of course enterprising publishers and unenterprising, thorough and careless, and like anyone else they have good days and bad days. But a manuscript, or part of a manuscript, or just a synopsis, backed by a simple letter explaining the purpose of the book and the readership in mind, your qualifications, previous publications and other relevant facts, will in most firms on most occasions receive the consideration it deserves, and no amount of oral persuasion will make a jot of difference. But make sure you give the publisher all the facts: have you had a previous book published by another firm or do you have evidence of a growing public interest in your subject?

BUILD A PARTNERSHIP

Let us suppose that you have chosen your publisher, that you have submitted an outline of the book and a specimen chapter which he likes, with or without amendments, and that you have agreed to complete the book by a certain date. An increasing number of books are now arranged in this way. The publisher usually issues a contract after seeing the sample, but the contract may contain a protective clause (at least if you are a new author), such as 'subject to the publisher's acceptance of the completed manuscript', so that he does not commit himself to publishing your work should its quality be below that of the sample. (Contracts and financial matters are dealt with in the two following chapters.)

If you are working for a publisher along these lines, ideally you should seek to build up a partnership. Both partners should accept their responsibilities and seek to develop the potential in the other. Both sides should immediately notify the other if there is any basic change of plan—the author if he meets with an accident or is promoted and moves, if he finds a massive new source of information, or if anything else happens to disrupt his schedule, the publisher if he wants to change the proposed plans in any substantial way—as he may occasionally have good reason to do.

If a book has been commissioned for delivery a year or two hence, an occasional progress report (say once every six months) may be welcomed by the publisher or even sought by him, especially nearer to completion date. If the author is unhappy or in difficulties with a certain aspect of his book, the publisher should be pleased to receive warning in good time and to be given the opportunity to offer advice (and perhaps arrange a meeting with the author). If the author is preparing roughs for maps, it will be sensible for him to check that the publisher likes a sample. The unexpected appearance of a rival book on the same subject might be another occasion for an exchange of letters, to explore the possibility of changing the emphasis of the new book so as to lessen duplication. If the subject suddenly becomes topical, it may pay to see if completion and publication can be expedited.

All publishers and authors should welcome such communications with a purpose. The author however should realise that though he may find nothing more fascinating than writing letters about his book, the publisher will be more matter of fact, having seen books written before. Curiously, the authors who write the longest and most frequent letters are often those slowest to get down to the actual grind of completing the book itself. It is the book that the publisher is waiting for, not a pile of correspondence about the difficulties of writing it or promises about its ultimate quality. Keep necessary letters short and to the point. Long and complicated ones may not get properly read and digested, and essential information or requests may therefore be overlooked—especially if the letter is hand-written. These days virtually all business is done by typewritten letters, and a long, handwritten scrawl will almost certainly be the last item examined in the mass of paper arriving by that day's post.

Conversely, some authors not merely lack the courtesy to tell their publisher when something goes wrong, but even ignore enquiries about what has happened to their overdue manu-script. If delays or difficulties arise and your publisher asks what has happened, the situation must be explained, warts and all; at least he should be able to offer constructive sympathy instead of sourly writing you off as a dead loss. A high credi-bility rating is one of an author's most valuable assets, and false promises and dour silences may be paid for dearly later.

WAITING FOR THE PUBLISHER'S REACTION

Your manuscript is complete, and you duly send it to the publisher. What should you now expect from him? Some kind of immediate acknowledgment should reach you, but this is no clue to the publisher's reaction. The editor concerned may indeed be on holiday, or working through a queue of waiting manuscripts, or feel that he needs to consult a colleague or out-side expert before making any personal comment, even if the book has been commissioned.

Reading a book in manuscript form, and studying illustra-tions, takes time and concentrated energy, and in smaller firms has to be fitted in by a few top people who also deal with much of the daily routine of publishing as a whole. Some degree of patience is required, and this is not the time to start writing letters, least of all to correct minor mistakes which may be discovered after the manuscript was posted; a chance to put these right will occur later and loose slips of 'add copy' are merely a nuisance now.

Ultimately, of course, anyone may have justification to hint that he has been kept waiting for too long. But if your patience will stand it, keep quiet for two months. There is no excuse for publishers to prevaricate unnecessarily, and a delay of more than two months before giving at least a first reaction should score a bad point against the firm. But it does of course depend on the length and complexity of your work, and allowances have to be made for the inevitable hazards of Christmas, summer holidays, illnesses, postal strikes and so on.

If your manuscript suddenly arrives back by post without warning, read the accompanying letter before becoming despondent. It has not necessarily been rejected, since even if the publisher is basically enthusiastic he may ask you to change the emphasis here and there, to reduce the length to the agreed number of words if you have written far too much, to supplement a thin patch or to check certain facts. (Since one of my firm's authors spent a week of gloom assuming we had rejected his book before he eventually opened the parcel and found it had been accepted subject to certain mild conditions, we have tried always to send a letter before returning manuscripts we like.) Once the manuscript is accepted, almost certainly you will get it back before the printer sees it; if it returns at this early stage, it will be because the publisher has some points he wishes you to reconsider before it goes to the sub-editor. As said earlier, publishers are not infallible, but their experience with books is greater than that of individual authors, especially new authors; they rapidly spot any section which let down the standard of the book as a whole, and the probability is that their requests for you to make certain changes will be justified—commercially, prestige-wise or both. Of course you will want to consider these requests seriously, especially if they involve a substantial amount of rewriting, but make sure of your ground before you dig in your toes and refuse to co-operate.

Sooner or later your book will be sub-edited. Different firms mean differing things by the term sub-editing, but it usually involves house styling where the author has not done it himself, smoothing of ugly sentences and corrections of grammatical errors. It may go further and include the rearrangement of certain passages into a more logical sequence, and even the complete revision of some pages, this being more likely if you are an amateur author and the publisher does not feel you have the capacity or professional touch to make these more drastic changes yourself. Questions of libel or offensive matter will be raised by the sub-editor, who may also ask the author to check on certain facts and make other suggestions—whether or not the main editor has already asked for one set of changes.

If the sub-editing is purely of a detailed nature and the author has already had the manuscript back to make any more radical changes, all should then be ready for printing. But if the sub-editing involves substantial revision, the author should certainly be asked to make a final check through the manuscript; in effect this means asking him to agree to the changes, and now is the moment to raise any specific objections to what the sub-editor has done. Again the author should consider changes and suggestions on their merit and not oppose them on principle; but if anything has been cut out that you urgently want left in, you should discover the fact and point it out, since the publisher will assume that you have accepted the manuscript as you return it to him and will not be pleased for you to 'restore' a sentence on an already full page at proof stage. It helps if the author uses a coloured ink for any final changes so that the sub-editor can check that these weave in satisfactorily and make no departure from the consistent house style.

TIMETABLES AND PROOFS

After sub-editing, there will inevitably be a long gap before the next stage: proofs. Just how long a gap depends on many

factors—how quickly your chosen publisher is used to working, whether a suitable sub-editor is available, what other books
in the same series or books potentially competing for the same
market may be in the pipeline already, how busy the printers
are. A happy standard timetable once the finished manuscript
has been accepted and if necessary amended by the author
might be:

January   Manuscript sent to sub-editor.

March   Sub-editing completed and manuscript returned
to author for final check.

April   Manuscript sent by publisher to printer (on a
date arranged with the printer back in say February, meaning that the timetable would immediately have gone wrong
had the author not completed his final check within a reasonable period.)

June   Proofs received by publisher and sent on to author.

July   Three or four weeks after proofs are received, they
are returned to the publisher and returned by him to the
printer, the index following a few days later and of course
having to be proofed separately.

August   Completed flat sheets sent by the printer to the
binder.

September   Bound copies available from the binder.

November   Publication, a minimum of four and more
usually six weeks after the delivery of the bound copies.

It can be done more quickly. My own firm published *The
Wreck of the Torrey Canyon* as a hardback book complete
with maps and plates just three months after the tanker hit the
rocks; but that kind of schedule involves overtime for both the
publisher and his printer, and wear and tear, and dislocation
of other projects only justified by extreme topicality. It can
be done far more slowly, and often is. It may be sensible to
elongate the schedule because the book concerned would be
best published in a particular month; for a guide book the best
publication month might be January or February and there

would be no point in rushing for October publication even if the manuscript were edited in March as in the example quoted. And publishers have to balance their lists, not bringing out too many books in total or too many in the same field, at one time. The example is anyway based on straightforward books going without hitch at any stage straight into page proofs. If heavy editing, or the additional galley-proof stage has to be added, at least another two months will normally be needed.

An efficient publisher should tell his authors when they may expect proofs and what kind of proofs, and when they must be returned duly corrected if the publication schedule is to be kept. He should also give warning if the forecast date of arrival of proofs is not going to be met, because the printer is running late. For his part, an efficient author should keep time free for the proofing period, and do his best to meet the publisher's date for the return of the proofs. If he cannot meet it, he should say so at once. If you cannot make your own index, the publisher will probably be able to arrange for it to be done for you, but he must be given adequate time to do so since professional indexers plan their work well ahead and may not have the required dates free.

Production schedules, which tie down each operation not just to a specific month but to an actual day within that month, are not made for fun. They seek to secure an orderly progression of work and to make the best use of the publisher's and the printer's resources. If proofs are returned late, even by ten days, publication on the chosen date may prove impossible. The printer who has kept one period free for handling your book may not be able to handle it ten days later, since another book will be scheduled to go on the machine then. Even if he can print your book just the ten days later so that the proposed publication date is kept, sales may suffer since advance copies will not be available so far ahead and the publisher's representatives will find their task harder.

Normally an author will be allowed two to three weeks to read and correct each set of proofs, and be expected to supply an index within a week of returning the page proofs. That will often mean hard, concentrated work, and planning well ahead. For instance, if the author wants a colleague in a different part of the country to comment on the proofs, time could be saved by asking the publisher to send a copy direct.

As well as returning the proofs and the index on time, they should be presented in a businesslike manner. It goes without saying that proof corrections should be kept to the minimum (see appendix 2), and this includes helping the publisher and printer by minimising changes even where the printer himself has slipped, though obviously any real mistake or omission has to be rectified.

A publisher who keeps to his part of the bargain and who uses a printer whose general standard of work is high deserves such support as you can give him. But if you have waited a year or more for proofs, and they then arrive without notice, and contain many stupid errors, your annoyance will be understandable. Make allowances, however, for the fact that while you are probably only dealing with a single book, the publisher will have many on his schedule and must regulate the progress of the book. No doubt publishers do not always bother to explain what is happening and why, and that of course is regrettable; but they will have their own ways of doing things and you may have to abide by them in the same way that you must in Britain drive clockwise round a roundabout. But do all in your power to make your publisher give adequate guidance and direction. If he does not volunteer proofing and publication dates, press him for them. Warn him if you are going on holiday a fortnight after the proofing period. A month before the proofs are due, check if they will be coming on time.

PUBLICITY

One matter tends to cause a quite disproportionate amount of trouble. That is the question of when and how an author should tell his publisher about his views on the way his book should be publicised, sold and generally exploited.

The new author often itches to get started on the publicity campaign and bombards the publisher with suggestions even before the manuscript is finished. He may then be irritated, perhaps months later, to be asked for the information all over again by the publisher, who possibly expects it all to be set out on a formal questionnaire. The author may reply that he has given the information already; he may give part of it again, but in his rush or irritation forget the rest and subsequently ask the publisher to consult previous letters. It does take some application to sit down and pour out information about yourself, your contacts, the societies that might be interested in the book, and so on, all at one go. But it must also be obvious that it is impossible for the publisher to build up an adequate picture unless he has some system, and that while the publicity department may not want to know about a book to be published twelve months hence, when the time comes to consider the campaign the staff do genuinely need *all* the information at once. Many a sale has been lost, many a reprint failed to be required, because some essential aspect of promotion has not been revealed or considered at the proper time or has been lost in letters chiefly concerned with other matters; at least occasionally this has resulted from authors being unwilling to go over ground they reckoned they had previously covered, even though the letters concerned may have been sent to quite different people in the publishing organisation.

Many firms ask the author to write a draft blurb—the description, usually of 100–300 words, that goes on the front flap of the jacket and also appears (perhaps abbreviated) in the catalogue. The emphasis is on 'draft' since the publisher himself will usually revise what the author sends in, using his own judgment and his assessment of the book's market. But even if the author provides only the rough material, his help can be invaluable in summarising just what his book has aimed to do. The blurb is, of course, intended to tell a potential purchaser in a bookshop just what the book is about; it should not be a paragraph about the author himself. There may however be

G

room for some details about the author, possibly with a photograph, on the back flap. Most publishers welcome photographs of their authors to keep on file.

Authors are also usually invited to suggest which newspapers and magazines might usefully be given review copies;
a skeleton list of periodicals may be sent for guidance. Considered suggestions will be treated seriously, but to tick every
paper on the skeleton list shows only enthusiasm, not discretion. Most newspapers will only publish reviews of books
that have been sent to them officially, and publishers therefore
usually ignore requests to send second copies to journalists at
their home adresses, though if you happen to know a contributor to a particular paper there is no harm in mentioning the
fact and the publisher may pass on an appropriate hint when
sending the editor a copy. The publisher will probably decide
for himself which popular daily and Sunday papers are worth
a free copy, and will avoid wasting highly specialised books on
newspapers that never review them. Though the publisher
should consult *Willing's Press Guide* to ensure thorough coverage, the author's personal knowledge of specialist and regional
publications can be especially valuable in ensuring that no
vital gaps are left.

Publishers normally reckon to send out something between
twenty and fifty review copies of a non-fiction book costing
£2 or more, covering radio and television services as well as
the press. The more specialist the work, the smaller the number
of periodicals likely to review it. Conversely, however popular
the book's subject there must be some upper limit, since review
copies cost money—and, of course, will earn the author no
royalty. Do not assume that your publisher is at fault if you
hear that an editor has 'not received' a copy: editors sometimes lend or even sell copies of books they do not intend to
review, and then have to resort to the 'not received' line if the
author happens to ask directly if a review is going to be published. Publishers also receive many requests for review copies
from newspapers and magazines not on their lists: some get

their copies and useful publicity may result, but others are too clearly unsuitable papers whose editors or contributors are just begging a book for personal use. If a separate edition of your book is published in America, requests for review copies from the other side of the Atlantic will be passed to the American publisher.

Review copies are of course sent out early to enable editors to get the reviews written and set up by publication date. They may go out even before the author has his own copies, and this is not unreasonable since the author does not immediately need copies for practical purposes and he can indeed upset booksellers by showing his book to people too soon.

In addition to review copies, it sometimes pays to send free copies personally to prominent people with influence in your subject field. But, again, free copies and the carriage on them cost the publisher money, and requests should not be made lightly. You can only reasonably expect the publisher to send to someone who might usefully aid sales—not to somebody to whom you have promised a copy because he gave you help. It is customary for you to fulfil that obligation yourself.

The publisher may also ask for your views on advertising and a prospectus. It almost always pays to place at least small advertisements in specialist magazines and journals, and your personal knowledge of the most useful publications and positions within them will be welcomed. But an inch in the popular press may cost £25 and must earn £250 in sales to break even. Tell the publisher if you think good use could be made of a prospectus or some form of information sheet describing your book and including an order form: there might be societies willing to circulate copies to their members, and you yourself might be able to use a hundred or so personally. But many prospectuses are printed without adequate thought being given to their use and end in the wastepaper basket. If the publisher produces other books on the same or related subjects, he may find it more economic and effective to produce subject lists. Do not object to back-list titles being advertised along with your new book: it shows that the publisher takes care to keep his older titles alive and your work will benefit from the same treatment in due course.

SUBSIDIARY RIGHTS

Certain kinds of books lend themselves to serialisation or 'one-shot' extracts in newspapers and magazines, which may give useful publicity and boost ordinary sales as well as bring extra income—though over-long extracts of a specialised or regional book may give potential buyers too much of the content free of charge, and make them feel it is not worth buying the book itself. Most newspapers and magazines work well ahead, and early planning is needed.

The sale of special editions to America or of the American rights, and also the sale of the British paperback rights, are obvious ways of reaching more readers and bringing in more royalties: the financial aspects are considered in the next chapter. Translation rights are a different field; the author may know of some reason why his book could have an appeal in Scandinavia or Japan that might not occur to the publisher, and finance apart it is fun to have your book printed in another language. Book clubs open up another avenue: as well as the general ones there are specialists in certain subjects. There is also the possibility of film or television usage. Few non-fiction books lend themselves to full screen treatment, but occasionally the BBC make use of material for a programme inspired by a book or devised quite independently of it.

The author should pass all enquiries for such rights to the publisher, who will of course be entitled to keep a proportion of the receipts as laid down in the contract (see next chapter). Incidentally, beware of the television producer or other seeker of your information and help who wishes to make use of your book but does not offer to get in touch with your publisher or offer you a fee direct: some producers, no doubt working on tight budgets, hint that it will be in your interest to have your work publicised, but then make use of it without acknowledgement, perhaps because the context of the programme simply did not allow any form of 'plug' for the book.

AFTER PUBLICATION

After publication, it will probably be the publicity department that you will be itching to write to and to hear from. You may not think that your book has been adequately advertised, or you may have a last-minute brainwave for attracting more publicity. You may want to discover what reviews have appeared so far, or send in a copy of a review in a specialist magazine that your publisher may not have seen. Some of this kind of contact can be useful and enjoyable to both sides, though enthusiasm can run too far. Authors who want weekly reports on review coverage should subscribe to a press-cutting agency. Some publishers, incidentally, will lend newspaper clippings or send photostats. Good reviews should certainly be kept, in case they may prove useful in launching a new edition, though publishers vary widely in the importance they attach to reviews as a whole.

The author may also ask the publicity department about the book's sales, or write to the sales manager direct. He may point out that his book is missing from the shelves of an obvious specialist bookseller who should be stocking it; he may report complaints from his friends that the book cannot be bought anywhere in East Anglia or Scotland. Again, a certain amount of such contact can be useful, and good sales managers and their representatives who service the bookshops should welcome genuine hints and even criticisms of their performance. But it is all too easy for the author to get his facts wrong. Ask for the number of copies that have been sold on publication date, if you like, but do not put in another request before the first royalty statement arrives. Make sure that any complaints are backed by fact. Authors can grumble that their books are unobtainable in certain bookshops simply because they did not immediately see them on display—sometimes even when in fact they were displayed, if looked for in the right place. If you want to make sure, ask an assistant. But regularly to do the rounds of bookshops checking up on the display and sales of a book is distinctly not useful.

You will probably want to buy some copies yourself. The author usually receives six free copies and is allowed to buy more at trade terms (normally a discount of $33\frac{1}{3}$ per cent) subject to the strict understanding that he does not resell copies at less than the full published price (see chapter 9). When ordering books for your own use, do so in a separate formal note and not in a letter also dealing with other matters—a point that like many in this book sounds almost stupidly obvious yet needs making: many authors tack an order to the end of a letter addressed personally to the managing director or editor, or even begin a letter on editorial or publicity matters with a request for copies that amounts to an order. Most publishers are departmentalised organisations, their commercial and despatch departments often being in different buildings, perhaps in different towns, from the editorial offices, and letters containing mixed requests add unfairly to the burden of administration, and cannot be promptly processed. Nor is it 'wasteful' when two or three separate envelopes are sent to you from different departments on the same day: the time and organisation needed to bring together all communications to one person would cost far more than a postage stamp or two.

If the book starts off by selling well, you may figure that the publisher must be taking a substantial amount of money, and that you could do with some for your new car or household repairs. Do you ask him for a cheque in advance? It depends. Many contracts of course stipulate advance payments of some kind, but even so authors may hope for an additional interim payment if the initial sales are better than expected and if the next ordinary royalty-payment date is still a long way off. If some hundreds of pounds have been earned for you a month after publication and you would otherwise have to wait six months, then by all means ask and most firms will give the request sympathetic consideration. But the publisher is not obliged to pay before the stated day; also, even if the book has sold well it does not follow that the bookshops and wholesalers have yet settled their accounts. If you do get one lump-sum payment ahead of the date arranged, do not assume it will be a precedent for earlier payment. Each request has to be considered by a responsible person, and if granted an interim entry made in the ledger, a cheque drawn, and so on, which all costs extra money in itself.

ANOTHER EDITION

Many books of the kind dealt with here should sell through successive editions if well handled by the right publisher. If you are interested in long-term sales, you should of course have made this clear to your chosen publisher in the first place, and if the initial sales are promising remind him of your expectations a few months after publication, so that he does not accidentally let the type or blocks be destroyed. It is also well worth keeping an eye on the stock position as revealed by the royalty statements; do not hesitate to take the initiative in making appropriate suggestions when the first edition looks like selling out.

Your book may have become outdated, in which case you might be able to give the publisher the confidence he lacks by pointing out that you realise the fact, that you have substantial new material and that the interest in the subject is rising. It is not unknown for the second edition to sell better than the first, especially when a tactful gap of six or twelve months can be left without any copies available, to make sure that no old stock remains on booksellers' shelves.

Even if the first edition was printed by letterpress and the type has been destroyed, a reprint by photolithography might be easy enough. In such cases any lines containing corrections are reset and stuck down over the lines they replace in a copy of the first edition, or on reproduction pulls of the type that may have been thoughtfully taken for the purpose. It is therefore easy to change a date, or even to replace a ten-line paragraph by another of ten lines, but much more difficult to add or subtract lines. Any major changes in the subject will probably have to be covered in an additional chapter or in an entirely rewritten last chapter. The point has already been made that topical allusions and forecasts can seem ridiculously out of date very quickly and that all such potentially ephemeral material is best concentrated in one place, preferably the last chapter or a post-script, where it can be easily changed for any reprint.

Authors should of course record any mistakes found in the original edition and keep material for a possible reprint available. Even if the basic hardback edition has not sold well enough to make a reprint likely, there may be a paperback, bookclub, school or foreign-language edition which should be corrected and brought up to date. Let your wife or children know where your corrected master-copy is kept in case the information is needed when you are on an extended overseas tour or dead.

TO BE REMAINDERED

If, alas, the book has not sold well, the publisher may tell you he proposes to remainder it—to sell it off cheap. At this stage under the terms of the contract, most publishers offer the author copies at the reduced price and also the blocks and any other 'plant'. Do not too meekly assume that the book has no future. If the publisher is selling it off because he makes a habit of doing so, or has changed his policy or the nature of his list, perhaps as the result of a merger with another firm, it may well be that a quite different publisher could be persuaded to accept the book; especially in our early days when we were building our business, my firm very successfully rescued a number of excellent books abandoned by publishers whose policies had changed. Even if no interested firm can immediately be found, once your publisher has definitely informed you that he is disposing of your book it may be wise to buy in as large a stock from him as you can (unless they are of a highly topical or ephemeral nature, sooner or later copies of most books become scarce) and see that somehow the blocks are retained. Interest in the subject may revive, even if years pass before a second edition is possible. There are of course occasional books that prove utterly unsaleable, so be sure that your belief in your own work is realistic.

ANOTHER BOOK?

Your first book has been launched. Now do you write another? And if so, who publishes it?

Many publishers like to see the reception accorded an author's first book and if happy may themselves suggest a sequel—especially if the author has proved businesslike. Certainly any suggestion you make will be sympathetically received. Conversely, if any suggestion for a second book is promptly turned down without the publisher hinting at an alternative idea, was it because previously he found you difficult to work with—your first manuscript failed to come up to expectation and had to be extensively sub-edited or even partly rewritten at heavy cost, you were unhelpful over providing illustrations or proof correcting, or in some other way you stood out as an intransigent amateur? The publisher may be too polite to say so; he may think that even if he did tell you, and even if you did not take offence, you would still cause a disproportionate amount of trouble on future books.

But at least nine out of ten authors whose first books have done reasonably well would be welcomed in the list again if a good idea could be offered or found. Indeed, a close relationship with an author who produces a succession of books over the years is a most satisfying experience for a publisher. Continuity makes extremely good sense; you get to know the publisher, his staff and their ways, and you appreciate each other's problems and attitudes; they get to know you, and enjoy hearing about the progress of your children and your move to a new home or job. One of your books helps to sell another. The fact that you have produced a third or fourth title could be the crucial factor in persuading the publisher to reprint the first when it goes out of print. Bookshops find ordering easier if all an author's books come from the same firm.

Some young authors believe they should appear in as many different publishers' lists as possible in order to make a name for themselves. They are wrong. Of course, if you write a second book of a very different type, or if you receive a specific invitation to contribute a volume to an established series published by another firm, some break in continuity may be inevitable. But the really successful author normally has one main publisher, works closely with him, and only goes elsewhere when strictly necessary. He should confide in his main publisher, and expect to be kept in the picture about that publisher's other developments in the same field. He also expects his books to be given new editions whenever possible. If such an association does not work smoothly, then you have chosen the wrong firm in the first place, or possibly you are the victim of changed policy following a takeover and should switch all your future titles to another publisher and start creating confidence afresh.

7 Your Contract

HOW IMPORTANT?

PEOPLE'S REACTIONS vary sharply when confronted with a legal document. Some authors are eager to sign their contract for a new book without taking even a cursory glance at it. Others virtually rewrite the entire thing. Some place implicit trust in their publisher; others display the maximum suspicion, assuming him to be guilty of trying to cheat until he proves himself innocent. Some think it unwise or too risky to question something they genuinely dislike; others feel they might look amateurish if they did not bargain and 'try on' at least a modicum of changes. Finally, some sign in copperplate and get that signature witnessed even if not requested to do so, while some demonstrate their contempt for formalities by scrawling only their initials and then in the wrong place, missing the stamp over which they have been asked to sign.

On the whole too much rather than too little fuss is probably made about the kind of contract we have in mind here—an agreement between a publisher and an author over the arrangements for the publication of a single book. Of course the approach should not be slap-happy, important points should be carefully checked, and signing should be done over the appropriate stamp (at present 6d). But normally only the one book is concerned, which means that except in unusual cases the sum of money involved will be much less than in the sale of a house, for instance. Again except in unusual cases, many of the standard contingencies provided for in the contract will never apply—film rights in the case of a mathematical text-book, for example. And in any case the contract need not necessarily be regarded as the final word, since in practice changes are often later agreed between publishers and authors in the light of experience.

Most publishers have taken considerable care in the preparation of their skeleton contract, which is usually a printed form with spaces for the individual book's title, contents and terms to be completed in typewriting. But it is hard to produce any form of words that pleases everyone, and an inordinate amount of time can be wasted by authors questioning the validity of certain clauses more or less standard among all publishers. Some authors even submit the contract to their solicitor to vet, and again great waste of time can result from the solicitor querying something that is standard trade practice. The solicitor, remember, will be paid for his work, while the publisher will have to fit it into his daily routine. (Publishers do not usually have special legal departments; garages don't either, and a new car is likely to cost more than at least the first edition of a non-fiction book will earn in royalties.) So take into account that while the contract may have novelty value for you, it has none for your publisher. He will have to make sure that any change from standard procedures is understood and carried into effect throughout his organisation, which in itself can be expensive.

Personal experience is that whenever authors and solicitors get to work on redrafting clauses, they not only all choose different clauses to attack (if everyone condemned the same provision there would indeed be a case for amending the standard form), but have the supreme knack of missing the very points which could be most important in the long run. The publisher has the greater knowledge of publishing, and if he is really set on cheating you he may succeed for all the care you and your solicitor exercise in reading the contract and getting it amended. It is therefore the choice of publisher that is vital.

The Publishers Association has recently produced a draft standard contract for the guidance of its members, and this is included by permission, with explanatory notes, as appendix 1. Though most contracts have the same basic construction, obviously those of different firms reflect the character of their

lists, fiction publishers being especially concerned with subsidiary rights, publishers of specialist scientific works with
arrangements for illustrations, and so on.

TITLE AND CONTENTS

Some publishers like formally to agree on the exact title
before a contract is signed, and if this is done you may later
find it difficult to persuade him to use a different one that he
feels will make the book harder to sell. If a book is to appear
in a series, this fact may be stated in the contract, and that will
of course weaken your case if you later wish it to differ in some
substantial respect from the pattern for the series; the contract
may even stipulate that the work will only be published subject
to the agreement of the series editor.

Most contracts mention the length of the book, if it has not
yet been fully written, and if the agreed length is say 70,000
words you should satisfy yourself that you can produce something between 65,000 and 75,000 words without undue padding
or compression. Some publishers also like to decide the number
of illustrations at the contract stage. All this does not necessarily close the door to later negotiation, but clearly if you
have agreed to write the work in 70,000 words, and supply
16 pages of plates, you cannot insist that the publisher accepts
as it stands your completed manuscript of 120,000 words plus
photographs for 48 pages of plates. This example would in fact
about double the publisher's costs, and the market might well
not stand a book at twice the price even if it were twice as large.

TERRITORY AND RIGHTS

The author is usually expected to grant the publisher the
exclusive use of the book in a defined territory and for a
defined period of time. These points deserve close attention.

The defined territory might be the British Commonwealth
(occasionally minus Canada), or it might be the world minus
the United States, or the entire world. But with the kind of
book we have in mind the only major discussion will concern

the inclusion of the United States. Shall the British publisher be given world rights, or will the author or his agent try to sell the American rights separately?

If the British publisher does handle the American rights, he can either sub-lease them to an American publisher who will print his own edition, or he can print in Britain a special edition, complete with an American-style binding, bearing an American publisher's imprint. In the first case he will act as the author's agent, retaining a small proportion of the American royalties. In the second case the royalties will be tied to the price of the British edition but paid on what is known as a *net receipts* basis. Instead of the royalty being calculated on the full British selling price, it will be based on the receipts obtained by the British publisher for the sale of the special edition. To quote a common example, a 10 per cent royalty on a £2 book produces 20 pence (4s) a copy for the author. But if the British publisher sells a special edition to America, the American publisher is likely to pay rather less than 40 per cent of the British price, say 75 pence (15s) per copy, and the author will then normally receive 10 per cent of this 75 pence, or $7\frac{1}{2}$ pence (1s 6d).

This $7\frac{1}{2}$ pence may not seem much, but a number of important factors should be borne in mind. Firstly, unless the book is going to have an extremely wide demand in the United States (see next page), the only economic way for an American publisher to sell it is to buy in copies from the British publisher. Secondly, because the British and American copies can then probably be printed together, with economies of scale, it may be possible to drop the price of the British edition, or to increase its size or quality, which might be in the long-term interest of the book and its author. Thirdly, the American publisher will buy in bulk. If the book is not of narrow British-only interest he may take, in a single transaction, as many copies as are sold to all British and other outlets in the first six, twelve or eighteen months, so that even if the amount of royalty per copy is low, a useful sum is produced at an early stage—and royalty will have been paid even if the American publisher does not succeed in selling all the copies. Fourthly, even though the American publisher may buy a sizeable first edition, if it sells well he may come back for repeat quantities, and if he does so when the British edition is running low, this may result in earlier reprinting—which may mean that home sales benefit from a more up-to-date version. Sometimes, indeed, a repeat American order is the one point which persuades a British publisher to reprint for home sales as well.

Especially in the case of straightforward books without many illustrations, and of substantial American interest, an author or his agent may sometimes do better by retaining the United States rights and foreign-language rights, and therefore remaining free to approach overseas publishers direct, and receiving all the royalties on those other publishers' editions. But selling overseas rights demands substantial know-how which few individual authors are likely to possess, while the British publisher may be itching to use his contacts. The greater the part the publisher has played in helping create and process the book, and the more complex the physical production, obviously the more he will want to control world rights and to achieve economy of production by printing all English-language copies in a single operation.

However, where there is a substantial American interest, a useful compromise is sometimes adopted: the book is printed separately by an American publisher but using the typography of the British edition. This means that the British publisher sells his American counterpart 'reproduction pulls' (high-quality proofs) of the text and illustrations. This has the advantage to the author that the American royalties are based on the full American published price, while the British publisher of course recoups part of his editorial and production costs, and if he knows that he is going to do so this may still enable him to pitch the published price of his own edition lower and so possibly increase home sales. Advance planning is obviously useful, since American publishers have their preferences and whims and these can be taken into account when the British publisher designs the book and sets up the type. Except for children's books, English spellings are fortunately acceptable to the American market even in books specially printed for it.

Thus while the agent of an internationally-famous novelist obviously has a strong case for retaining all the rights he can in his own hands, make sure that neither you nor your agent spoil all possibility of winning an American sale by refusing to allow your British publisher the right to sell copies or to co-operate in some other way (such as sharing the cost of editorial work and typography) with an American publisher. Remember that if only 1,000 copies can be sold in America anyway, then the British publisher is the only person who can produce them economically. Not only that, but he himself may only be able to do so while he is printing the British edition, so that if you try to find your own American publisher and fail, it may be too late to do anything.

Against this, watch that the British publisher does not prematurely sell a special edition to America or elsewhere out of copies that were originally destined for ordinary sale. If the demand for the ordinary edition has effectively ceased, it is obviously good sense to meet say a repeat American order out of remaining stock; but the author gets a bad bargain if the publisher succumbs to the temptation of a quick special-edition sale (yielding a low royalty) and thus runs out of copies for home sales (yielding full royalty). A safeguard in the contracts used by some agents is that the British publisher has to commit himself to printing so many copies of the ordinary edition for full-royalty sales, and any special-edition sale to America or to a bookclub has to be on top of that figure. But the author's greatest safeguard is to start by picking a publisher who would normally reprint a book that went out of print quickly and whose interest is not solely in the short-term gain.

Many contracts devote much space to the question of subsidiary rights. With fiction and other literary types of work, the sales of subsidiary rights may prove extremely rewarding; some novels are published solely for the rights income they are likely to generate. But subsidiary rights are usually less important with definitive non-fiction, and the contracts of publishers specialising in such works or educational books may cover the whole subject in a single sentence. The author should check that he will receive at least three-quarters of any income from the translation of the work into a foreign language, or at least half of the income from a serialisation or extract published in a newspaper or magazine.

Paperback rights are obviously more important. They are almost invariably controlled by the publisher of the hardback, who expects to split the income 50-50 between himself and the author. On the whole this is fair. That there is a demand for the book in paperback form may be due to his original success in promoting the hardback edition, whose sales may suffer once the cheaper version is on the market. But authors of definitive non-fiction should remember that it is almost always the hardback that accounts for most of the income. Unfortunately some publishers who let the original hardback edition go out of print not only still expect to enjoy the paperback income but are unwilling to relinquish the hardback rights. The author is then in a cleft stick, receiving no hardback royalties and only half the less rewarding paperback ones.

TERM OF CONTRACT

Especially in these days of takeovers and changes of policy, perhaps the most vital clauses in contracts are those relating to what happens when the original hardback edition goes out of print. Ideally authors should seek the return of *all* rights to themselves if the hardback edition goes out of print and the publisher declines to reprint it within a reasonable period. But the appropriate clause now more usually reads 'If the work shall become out of print and not be available in any edition issued by the Publisher or authorised by him', while some publishers in fact reckon to reserve the right to sell all rights in

H

perpetuity (including even the hardback rights to another hardback publisher in due course) of any book they have once had in their list.

Once more, the best protection the author can give himself is to choose a publisher who will not let a worthwhile book still in demand go out of print indefinitely, or who if he does not feel able to reprint will have the grace to release all rights, or at least the income from them. See how the contract for your book is worded in this important respect. Do not, however, be too harsh on the publisher regarding the length of period he may request before the rights revert to you, if no reprint is produced, for there are a variety of reasons why it may pay to delay a reprint. Some agents seek to have rights revert to the author if the work remains out of print for only six months; two years seems a more reasonable time, since a judicious gap between editions may be beneficial or the publisher may want to delay slightly to prevent clashing with other titles in the same series or on the same subject.

Another essential point to check is the period that must elapse before the publisher can produce a cheap edition, or remainder or otherwise dispose of the stock. Two years is not an unreasonable minimum before any consideration should be given to reducing the price of the hardback edition, even though the author will probably be wise to agree to the production of an additional bookclub or other special edition at a lower price. Experience shows that very rarely indeed do bookclub or other *special* editions hurt the sale of the main hardback edition, and if they produce relatively little revenue (royalties again normally being calculated on a net-receipts basis), at least it is extra; but any drop in the price of the main hardback edition, even temporarily as for a book sale, can irrevocably damage future prospects. As said in the last chapter, most contracts enable the authors to buy copies of the book and blocks and other plant should the publisher feel that the demand has ceased and want to remainder or even destroy the remaining stock. This protection can be extremely useful where the publisher has lost interest as the result of change of ownership or policy.

But first there should be at least a modest period of sales! Having discussed the extent of the publisher's rights, both geographically and in time, the remaining contract points can perhaps be best discussed under the headings of the author's and the publisher's responsibilities.

THE AUTHOR'S RESPONSIBILITIES

The author will be expected to confirm that the work is his own property, that if any copyright permissions are needed he will obtain them, that there is nothing of a libellous or scandalous nature in his manuscript, and normally that he will indemnify the publisher against any actions or costs should the work be imperfect in any of these respects.

A useful note on the copyright law of both Britain and America is included in *The Writers' and Artists' Year Book,* but here we may briefly note that ordinary British copyright persists for fifty years after the death of the author. Normally a very short extract of copyright material may be used to demonstrate a point without the need to obtain copyright permission. For more substantial extracts permission must be obtained, especially if they are quoted for their own sake rather than as a (properly acknowledged) reinforcement of your argument. Most publishers expect authors to provide photographs at their own expense, again with any copyright complications cleared. As stated in an earlier chapter, the publisher may make a contribution to the author's costs in clearing copyright fees.

The Writers' and Artists' Year Book also contains a note on the law of libel, but one essential point to remember is that a statement does not necessarily have to be untrue to be libellous; a man's reputation and business may be damaged by the circulation of a perfectly true statement. Only in very special cases is it worth running the risk of libel proceedings; if in any doubt leave out the passage concerned. Where there is some overriding reason for the inclusion of a statement you feel could possibly constitute libel, then explain it when you send the manuscript to the publisher.

Increasingly contracts stipulate that authors should type their manuscripts in accordance with the publisher's house style, and that they should submit two copies of the completed manuscript. Some publishers specify that the manuscript shall be presented in a suitable condition for going straight into page proofs: in other words it must be the *final* manuscript. Rising costs and new techniques will make this kind of stipulation ever more common. For some books a few publishers are already asking their authors to ensure that the typescript is accurate to the extent that no proofs need be rendered. This usually means that film-setting is being employed. Film-setting bypasses the use of heavy, hot-metal cast type, and if all goes smoothly may be considerably cheaper; but corrections are difficult and costly, so that the publisher must ensure that there is not a long delay between the author finally checking the manuscript and publication. Publisher and printer will of course check that the printed version exactly follows the author's copy.

Other responsibilities the author usually carries are to read and return proofs within a stated period (often three weeks), to make the index, and to undertake revisions to the book from time to time should new editions be required. The contract will normally be worded so that the publisher can deduct from the royalties the cost of having these operations done should the author fail to do the work himself. Indeed, most contracts go so far as to say that if the author does not complete the book itself by the due date the publisher may get it completed and deduct the cost from royalties or other monies due to the author. Such intervention is of course extremely rare, and though authors should try to honour their delivery dates, most publishers are long-suffering. Eventually, if the author fails to deliver the manuscript, and more particularly if he refuses to say what progress he has made and when he hopes to complete it, the publisher may give notice that he intends to cancel the contract. But this happens only in extreme cases. When the author of an existing book that needs revising is dead or infirm, or positively wishes someone else to do the work, the publisher may engage a suitable substitute and deduct the cost from royalties.

Finally, the author may be asked to give the publisher an option on his next one or two books. The option clause usually states something like: 'The Publisher shall have the first option of reading and the first option of publishing the Author's next work on terms to be agreed with the Author.' Since the author can anyway reject any terms offered him, the clause really does no more than say that the author should keep his publisher informed about his next book or books. New authors should have no hesitation in accepting this. Even established authors who ask for the clause to be deleted because they have already committed work elsewhere should keep their publishers informed about their plans. If no more, this may prevent you waking up one morning to see that your original publisher has produced a sequel to your first book written by your professional rival in competition to your second work which you have taken elsewhere. If an author writes a number of different types of book, he sometimes asks for the words 'of the same kind' or 'on the same subject' to be inserted, qualifying the option so that he is free to take other works elsewhere.

THE PUBLISHER'S RESPONSIBILITIES

The publisher normally undertakes to look after the manuscript and other material with reasonable care, but he gives warning that he is not an insurer and the risk of loss or damage is the author's.

The publisher normally guarantees to produce the book within a certain time after the delivery of the complete manuscript and illustrations, but the author's degree of protection is usually whittled away by the addition of such words as 'unless prevented from doing so by circumstances beyond their control'. The circumstances beyond the control of certain publishers may of course be sheer bad planning. Many books that should have been published within twelve or eighteen months of the delivery of the manuscript do not appear for thirty-six or even forty-eight months, for no better reason than that nobody has come round to attending to them. Yet again, try and choose an efficient publisher. If you are unlucky, remember this clause and press the publisher to say what particular circumstances have been beyond his control; but press early, since if you hear nothing at all for two years it could just be that nothing has happened and that all still has to be done.

Most agreements spell out the fact that the whole of the physical production of the book shall be controlled by the publisher, and that he can determine the price charged for it, how many free copies are used to promote its sale, and so on. In return, of course, the publisher normally accepts the whole of the risk of the venture, the author's financial liabilities being limited to excess proof corrections; he is normally charged for any changes he makes in excess of 10 per cent of the original cost of composition. Since corrections are infinitely more expensive than original composition, this 'free' allowance of 10 per cent does not in fact buy very much, though the correction of printer's errors will not count: use a different-coloured pen to mark these.

The contract of course states what remuneration the publisher is to make to the author. Finance (including rates of royalties) is dealt with within the next chapter. The only point that needs mentioning here is the date on which royalties become payable. In the past they were almost universally paid half-yearly; today many firms reduce their book-keeping by making only an annual payment. On the whole this change is fair; it is in everyone's interests that overheads are kept to a sensible minimum. But if the publisher proposes to pay only once a year and your book should miss the first payment date by an odd month or two, you will have a long wait unless you ask for interim settlement, say three or six months after publication. Some publishers who normally pay yearly will willingly amend a contract to allow for half-yearly payments in the first one or two years. Any interim payments may be based on estimated sales and not on carefully checked stock and sales records. Also in an effort to keep down costs, many firms do not now make payments if the amount due is less than a certain minimum, usually £2.

The publisher states he will give the author so many free copies (usually six) and offers further copies at his usual trade terms, and perhaps even offers any book in his list at these terms, all on the understanding that you do not contravene the Net Book Agreement (see chapter 9). The clause about free copies causes publishers a quite disproportionate amount of correspondence, since many authors write to ask if the six can be increased to seven, eight, nine, twelve, twenty or a hundred. Ingenious are the reasons given to back these claims; most are rejected. Publishers exist to *sell* books! Anyway they like to be fair between authors. If you want to buy fifty or more to give away to people who have helped you, the publisher may be prepared to allow special terms. Only if there are joint authors is the number of free copies normally much increased, and then only to prevent time-wasting triangular correspondence!

JOINT CONTRACTS

From the last remark it may be judged that joint contracts, involving more than one author, are unpopular with publishers. The number of letters that have to be written and the number of queries that have to be answered seem to rise disproportionately to the number of people who have a hand in the writing.

Before you become a 'joint author' make sure it would not be as easy to do the whole job yourself, or at least to take the prime responsibility, the contract with the publisher being in your name, even if you do sub-contract certain parts to someone else and acknowledge that help on the title page or elsewhere.

In fact it is not unduly difficult to arrange a contract jointly in two people's names, each of them to be paid half the royalties. Problems begin to get serious when three or more are involved. Not only is there the matter of dividing royalties (perhaps small amounts years after the book has been published) into fractions, recording all the authors' changes of addresses, and so on, but the more people involved, the more they change their minds, and the more the likelihood of life's natural hazards hitting one of them. Seldom does a work planned with half a dozen joint authors come smoothly to fruition, all delivering their parts by the agreed date.

Put bluntly, a book by a number of different authors is less likely to get published than a comparable work by one or perhaps two. If there has to be more than a single author, the most efficient plan is for one alone to act as editor, or at least as spokesman, for the contract to be made with him, and for him to make private arrangements with the others—all that the others need is a formal exchange of letters with the leader to protect their position. Failing any agreement of that kind, the publisher may have no alternative but to purchase the work of the individual contributors outright, though perhaps still paying a small royalty to the chief author or editor. The problem in selling work outright is that the incentive interest for the contributor is removed and neither the publisher nor you can know what sum should be paid. If there are ten contributors, £50 apiece might seem mean, and would indeed be mean if the book ran through several editions; yet £500 might be a higher sum (in addition to an editor's royalty) than the publisher would normally lay out on the copyright of a specialist work.

LATER USE

You may seldom have occasion to glance at your contract once your book has been published, or once it has gone out of print and seems to be dead. But you or your descendants could possibly want it many years later.

As said earlier, British copyright expires fifty years after the author's death, and many authors publish their best books when they are still relatively young. Books which enjoyed only a modest success when they appeared in the 1910s, 1920s and 1930s are being confidently reprinted to-day, the authors' descendants drawing the royalties—though in some cases the reprinting publishers find it hard to trace those descendants (especially if the original publishers have ceased business) and the original contracts never come to light. The loss of the contract should not in itself prevent republication, of course, but if available it might clarify an issue otherwise uncertain. Its existence might act as a reminder that you once published a certain book or books and so encourage your children or grandchildren to take steps to keep your name and ideas alive and receive some belated income for themselves.

The best place to keep your contract is with your will, which itself should mention your copyrights. Make your instructions as specific as possible. Even if any royalties are to be divided equally between a number of beneficiaries, can you nominate one to have power to act on behalf of all in dealings with publishers? Joint executors scattered round the world and perhaps with no knowledge of publishing practice are even more unpopular with publishers than living joint authors.

8   Authorship and Finance

NOT PURELY FOR MONEY

BOOKS SHOULD NOT be written *solely* for money. If your objective is to make large sums quickly, there are easier ways of doing it than through authorship. Conversely, if you specifically want to write a book, whether because you have something to communicate or because you wish to build up your reputation in some field, you will have views on how it should be done and will take more than minimal care over it; you will not be making money the sole criterion of the project's value.

Publishers learn to beware of the author who says he has no other interest in book-writing than earning money—and of the would-be author who starts by placing undue emphasis on requesting the financial 'low down'. Books from such people are usually superficial. They do not sell well. They are bad bargains for their publishers and they do not enhance their writers' prestige.

The public is far more discriminating than most newcomers to authorship and publishing perhaps believe. Good books genuinely do a lot better than bad ones. But it takes time to sort out the wheat from the chaff. The quality of the work may not make much difference to the size of initial orders or indeed perhaps to the sales during the whole of the first year. Thereafter the gap widens, the potboiler dying a natural death while the quality work settles down to a steady sale month by month, year by year, perhaps with occasional fillips as new and revised editions appear.

FULL OR PART-TIME AUTHORSHIP?

The problem is that at the end of the first year after publication, which probably means two years since he completed the writing, and perhaps three years since he incurred the cost of much of the research, the thorough and competent writer may have received no greater royalties than if he had skimped the job. At this stage, therefore, his rate of payment per hour of work spent on the book will be positively less than had he rushed it. And if he is in a precarious financial position, such as having just married and bought a house, it may be no vast comfort to know that he will still be drawing royalties from the sale of his book when his first child gets married.

But there is no disputing the fact that responsible authorship of non-fiction books of the kind discussed here demands taking the long-term view. This means that the young man desperate for immediate spending money should not be writing a book at all, but selling his time some other way. His book may anyway be better if he can delay starting it till he is under less pressure. It also means that it is hard for anyone, however talented, to turn authorship successfully into a full-time profession.

The part-time author whose basic salary is provided by another job can afford to invest in his book, perhaps receiving the fruits of his labour spread over five, ten or even fifty years. If he writes a succession of books in his spare time, eventually he may receive substantial yearly royalties to supplement his basic income, and he may be in the happy position of knowing that these royalties will continue after he retires from his basic job, and that it would not matter unduly even if he lost that job or retired early.

But except for a very small handful of famous people, full-time authorship is apt to be a grinding struggle to make ends meet. The man who lives by his writing has somehow to keep himself and his family—who are not likely to be content with a low standard of living—and is obsessed with his short-term financial problems. He cannot write what he would most like to write since that will not produce enough spending money. He is liable to be so taken up with today's financial problems that he cannot invest in the scholarly work that might assure him of a steady income five years ahead. In five years' time he will still be battling to make immediate ends meet. But by then his publisher (or publishers, for he usually has to be prolific enough to need several) may realise that he is producing a succession of potboilers.

There are nominally full-time authors who do not have to worry unduly about immediate money matters since they enjoy a private income or their wives or husbands earn the bread and butter. But except for the top 1 per cent (who will not be reading this book anyway) and those with other income, full-time authorship is not on. So often one has seen the man who sought freedom in a freelance life become slave to the routine of writing what he does not want to write in order to keep the wolf from the door. Not only do his books tend to become potboilers, mere re-hashes of his own and other people's previous works, but he is forever snatching at opportunities in journalism, broadcasting and lecturing to supplement his income, and may actually end up with less time (and less creative energy) for writing books than he would have if he gave five working days a week to some other job.

The best advice to the would-be author is to remain with a congenial job in some walk of life that will not use precisely those parts of his being that authorship demands. The journalist is potentially the worst of authors for the fairly solid type of book; however practised his ability to communicate and marshal his thoughts, he cannot turn to writing his book with a fresh mind: the work is merely an extension of his daily job. The university lecturer or the school teacher, the accountant, civil servant, technician, industrial consultant or solicitor, even the manual worker, bring greater spontaneity; and in any case their daily work and contacts develop their experience and feed them with material and ideas for their writing. This alone gives them the advantage over the full-time author whose reservoir of thoughts and material—and capacity for sitting endlessly at his desk—is apt to run dry.

So if your first one or two books should be outstanding successes, do not fall into the common trap of assuming you can maintain that success for the rest of your working life. By all means plan to retire a few years earlier to devote more time to writing, or deliberately let promotion bypass you in your main job so as to retain adequate free time; but avoid the all-too-real possibility of having to churn out two or three pot-boilers year by year because you have no other source of income and each successive book you publish sells less well than its predecessor.

But of course take your book-writing seriously. Be professional in all respects except in depending on it exclusively for your livelihood. Be professional even in striking the most sensible bargain with your publisher!

METHODS OF REMUNERATION

Basically there are three kinds of arrangements between authors and publishers:

(1) The publisher takes the risk involved in publishing and pays the author a royalty based on sales.

(2) The publisher takes the risk but buys the author's copyright outright for a lump sum.

(3) The author and publisher share the risk, or the author bears the whole of it, with some kind of subsidy or profit-sharing arrangement.

Most adult non-fiction books published in Britain are covered by the royalty arrangement, which has much to commend it. Since both author and publisher have an interest in the continuing success of a book, they are encouraged to work closely together. The author's reward is linked not only to the book's sales but to the price at which it is published; that price may steadily increase over the years, as costs of production rise, giving him some protection against inflation.

If the author sells the copyright outright to the publisher, the purchase price is likely to be far less than royalties would eventually earn. The lure of £500 in outright payment when you need a new car or a world trip to gather material for the next book may be appreciable, but try to withstand it. Retain your equity stake in your creation. Remember that the interest in your subject may suddenly increase or there may be overseas or subsidiary-right possibilities that had not occurred to you; remember that if the book is reprinted for the British market the price of the second edition may be higher than that of the first. But the overriding objection to outright payments is perhaps that they are seldom equitable to both parties; either the publisher or the author is apt to feel he has had the bad end of the bargain—a feeling which does not help promote understanding if further books are to be produced. There are, of course, exceptions. Publishers of short books for children sometimes buy the texts outright on the grounds that the work involved for the writer was little more than jobbing journalism. The publisher of a symposium with ten contributors may want to pay a lump sum to each merely to ease the burden of administration—though even then the contributors might seek to retain certain rights, including perhaps freedom to use their own part in books of their own authorship at a later date.

The third kind of arrangement, involving the author in contributing to the costs of production, needs approaching with care. Competition for publishable books is intense, and if your book has any commercial potential, it should be possible to find a publisher to nurture it—maybe with payment of only nominal royalties, and maybe with fewer illustrations than you might have preferred, but still risking the sinking of some hundreds of pounds of his own money into the venture without asking you to contribute. If all likely firms (including perhaps a university press prepared to subsidise a few high-quality manuscripts of strictly limited appeal) turn you down on an ordinary royalty basis, the book should probably not be published at all, and if you do find a firm willing to produce it wholly or partly at your expense, you stand an excellent chance of losing your cash and of seeing that the other publishers were right in their decision not to risk theirs.

But, as to all rules, there are honourable exceptions. Printing is a mass-production process, and even a specialist publisher normally needs to be able to see a sale well into four figures before he can take the book into his list. There are some highly specialist books whose sales may never reach 1,000, or even 500, but which might nonetheless be welcomed by a small band of professional or other people. If the author has money to spare to support publication, there is no reason why he should not do so. But he must select a reputable publisher who does handle books in that subject field—a firm that would have been prepared to accept the work at its own risk had the sales potential seemed slightly greater. Ideally the author should only make a contribution to the expenses, or better still get a subsidy from a university or other organisation. He should study the contract carefully, making sure that the publisher will produce the book in the kind of way he wishes, and that adequate provision is made for the return of his contribution or for other payment in the event of the work selling well, however unlikely that may appear. He should consult his colleagues and also his wife, and should not try to persuade himself or them that his money will certainly come back—that his judgment is better than that of the publishers who have refused to accept the risk.

The author unable to get his work published in the ordinary way by a commercial publisher should be careful to avoid firms dealing mainly in sponsored works. Give £250 subsidy or loan to a reputable firm, conversant with the type of book concerned, and at least the book will be properly and suitably produced, and published and circulated exactly as any ordinary book in which publisher as well as author has faith. But this will not necessarily be achieved by some of those firms that specifically exist to 'publish' books at their authors' expense, often advertising their services in weekly newspapers. 'Publishing' in such cases often means little more than printing. True, the books are announced as being available for sale to the trade, but the trade knows that the author will have had to pay for the privilege of 'publication', which normally implies that no reputable publisher would accept the work at his own risk, or even with a subsidy, and that therefore the sales potential is negligible.

ROYALTY ARRANGEMENTS

One of the best-known facts about publishing is that the 'standard' rate of royalty is 10 per cent, based on the full published price, though the publisher sells at a substantial discount to the trade. But while 10 per cent is usual for a wide range of books, there is nothing immutable about it, and all kinds of circumstances have to be taken into account.

At the lower end of the scale, on specialist books, and especially on those with elaborate illustrations where the physical costs of production will account for a higher than average proportion of the published price, the royalty may start at $7\frac{1}{2}$ per cent or even 5 per cent, perhaps rising to 10 per cent after the sale of 1,000 or 2,000 copies. Alternatively the publisher may feel he can only accept the work subject to paying no royalty at all on the first 500 or 1,000 copies sold, and providing the position is clearly understood by the author, there is nothing necessarily wrong in that. Some authors volunteer to take lower royalties, or no royalties on sales up to a certain number, in order to persuade the publisher to include colour illustrations or some other feature that could not otherwise be afforded.

But on a conventional hardback published for the adult market the royalty should normally reach the standard 10 per cent after the sale of the first few thousand copies; some publishers who start with a lower royalty on the first batch of copies safeguard their authors by backdating royalty payments to 10 per cent on all copies should the book sell better than expected within a certain time. Such a provision might be worded: 'A royalty of $7\frac{1}{2}$ per cent shall be paid on the first 1,500 copies sold and of 10 per cent on all sales above 1,500 copies, but should 2,000 copies sell within the first year of publication then the royalty shall be calculated on the 10 per cent basis for all copies.' The argument behind this is that if the publisher has sold 2,000 copies in a year, he will most likely have recouped his working capital, and therefore has less excuse not to pay the 'standard' 10 per cent.

Most authors will probably not be offered a royalty greater than 10 per cent on their first book, but might ask for an increase on sales over a certain figure when the contracts for second and subsequent books are drawn up. On some types of books well-established authors may be paid say $12\frac{1}{2}$ per cent after 2,500 or 5,000 sales, and perhaps as much as 15 per cent after 5,000 or 10,000 copies. But again it depends on the type of book. The more expensive and complex the production, the less likely is the publisher to be able to afford anything over 10 per cent. Thus while a novelist may be offered 15 per cent on sales over 7,500 because the run-on cost of printing novels without illustrations is usually low, this rate may not be practicable in the case of a lavishly-illustrated book. The author of the latter does, however, have the satisfaction of knowing that his royalty is based on the higher published price necessitated by the more complex production. Royalty rates are not everything; income depends as much on the price of the book, 5 per cent of £2 being the same as 10 per cent of £1.

A lower rate of royalty is normally paid on export sales, and as has been mentioned in chapter 7, where the publisher sells copies at less than half the published price he usually pays a royalty on the basis of his 'net receipts' rather than the full published price. If the royalty rate is on a sliding scale, the point at which the higher percentage begins is normally calculated only on the ordinary home sales, export and special-edition sales at cheaper prices not being included. In other words if the royalty rate goes up to $12\frac{1}{2}$ per cent after the sale of 2,500 copies, the sale of a special edition to America of 2,000 copies will not be included in the 2,500.

Some publishers pay a flat fee to cover royalties on the first edition, paying ordinary royalties for the second and subsequent

K

editions. If the size of the edition is not stipulated, this encourages the publisher to produce the largest printing he dares. This may work against the author. Temptation to print unrealistically large first editions should particularly be avoided with books with a topical ingredient, since better overall sales might be achieved with successive smaller printings with revisions. Personally I dislike any change in royalty rate connected with change of edition. Especially with elaborate books that need bringing up to date, the cost of a second edition may be little less than that of the first, and a commitment to pay an increased royalty rate might make the publisher decide not to risk it at all.

As already stated, royalty rates are normally lower on paperbacks, and lower rates are also common with children's books and school textbooks designed to be sold in large numbers at low prices.

What about advances against the royalties the book is expected to earn? The author writing his first book may not be offered an advance, but established authors expect one. Advances may be paid on signing the contract, on delivery or acceptance of the completed manuscript, or on publication, or divided between two or three of these occasions. Normally only the famous professional author, or someone writing a book with enormous sales expectations, is paid an advance of any size on signing of the contract; with non-fiction books of the kind considered here the more normal arrangement might be an advance of £100 on delivery of the manuscript or of £50 or £75 both on delivery of the manuscript and on publication.

Publishers paying the largest advances are often those backed by big holding companies and so with access to reserves of ready cash; but these include firms that sometimes suffer from poor management and lack of individual concern for their books, therefore operating a fairly ruthless policy of not reprinting moderately successful books and of remaindering those that fall short of the sales target. Conversely, some of the best-run firms work on limited liquid-cash resources, and especially if they exploit long-term possibilities cannot afford to tie up too much money too far ahead of publication.

One final point: sometimes authors complain that their receipts are so small that publishers cannot notice paying them. This is not true. From the publisher's point of view it is perhaps unfortunate that royalties are calculated as a percentage of the full published price rather than as a proportion of their actual receipts. Thus while the author may receive only 10 per cent of the total money paid by the public on the purchase of his book, the publisher has to pay out a great deal more than 10 per cent of his receipts. Royalties are distinctly not a marginal consideration in publishers' balance sheets.

TAXATION

While tax inspectors make sure that their 'clients' declare all taxable income, they do not always check that every allowance or expense has been claimed. It is unfortunately just not enough to leave everything to the Inland Revenue. Indeed, not only do some inspectors refrain from pointing out what allowances could be claimed, but in their rush to complete cases they sometimes resist authors claiming allowances to which they are perfectly entitled. On the whole, tax-office staff are no doubt fair, but they are human, they are grossly overworked, and their performance varies.

I myself once naïvely took the view it was safe to leave matters to the Inland Revenue. (To quote my own case may help make the point more forcibly than a theoretic example.) I duly filled in my annual tax return, and sent it with a note of the expenses I had incurred in order to earn my income as a freelance author and journalist. I comfortably assured myself that I was being treated fairly, and was saving the cost of professional accountancy advice. It was only years later, when I also ran another business and needed an accountant to deal with its more complicated tax affairs, that I realised I had been paying an unnecessary amount of tax. For a start the accountant, who then took over the whole of my personal finances, succeeded (in a single exchange of letters) in making the inspector agree to something I had unsuccessfully pressed on a number of occasions. I had merely put forward a commonsense argument; the accountant quoted the exact wording of the relevant Finance Act to prove that what he was seeking was in accordance with the law.*

The emphasis is always on the law. Basic fairness and unfairness, and any consideration of ethics, do not really come into it. If the law is downright unfair and even unethical, you have to obey it. You also exploit its weak points. You cannot afford to pay up when the law is unfair to you, and also pay up when you feel it would be unethical to take advantage of a legal loophole or you cannot be bothered to make a claim that would involve some work. At any rate, if you do take the 'heads you win, tails I lose' attitude, do not blame your publisher for not paying you enough to make your writing worthwhile.

Since most authors do not have the time or inclination to follow closely the changes in taxation law and practice, and since the law becomes ever more complicated, almost certainly it will be worthwhile employing a professional accountant—ideally a partner in a smallish firm or branch office of a larger organisation who can give individual attention to the often quite complex tangle surrounding the financial transactions of publishing even a few books.

You might not feel it necessary to go to an accountant until the business of authorship really starts—say after the receipt of the first royalties. But whatever you do, make sure that you record all relevant expenditure from the very start of your project—while you are doing research, perhaps years before you actually put pen to paper. At worst these accumulated expenses will be offset against the income when it arises; at best they

* While this book has been in the press an editor was told by her tax inspector that she was not entitled to charge a certain expenditure but that in her case half of it would be allowed as a concession. After reference to an accountant the inspector then immediately conceded that she was entitled to the whole sum as of legal right.

should be offset against your other income even before you receive your first payment from your publisher, and a reduction in your current tax liabilities may give authorship greater point in the eyes of both yourself and your wife (or husband). The tax inspector will of course need convincing that you are genuinely set to become an author before he starts allowing expenses to be offset against your other income—merely dabbling with the possibility of writing will not suffice.

Two especially important points about taxation should be understood by authors not wanting to pay more tax than necessary. The first concerns the schedule under which the profits of authorship are taxed; the second the accounting period, or tax year.

How You Should Be Assessed   It is crucial that your activities as an author are assessed under Schedule D (which is for those engaged in a trade or profession on a self-employed basis), as opposed to Schedule E (for employees on a pay-as-you-earn basis.) Some inspectors of taxes try to get authorship and other freelance earnings reflected in the Schedule E assessment on the person's basic staff salary. One-twelfth of the assessed sum is then deducted from the salary each month, or one fifty-secondth part each week. The whole of the freelance fees are retained, but the person concerned receives a smaller part of his salary from his employer.

The objections to this are several and should be noted separately.

(*a*)   The Schedule E assessment is often rough and ready and though in theory you should pay exactly the amount of tax due, split equally between twelve months or fifty-two weeks, in practice a substantial final adjustment is often necessary, spoiling the point of trying to do it evenly.

(*b*)   You may well dislike your employer being able to guess at your authorship income or lack of it by having it reflected in your PAYE code number.

(*c*)   Expense allowances are more generous—distinctly so—

under Schedule D than Schedule E. The difference can scarcely be exaggerated. Under Schedule D you may claim allowances for any reasonable expense incurred in authorship, such as heating your office, hotel accommodation when visiting an area to collect material, or a salary you pay your wife to help you (see page 140). But under Schedule E you will be treated as an employee, and it will be little easier to convince your tax inspector that it was necessary to employ your wife to help with your book than that she was employed to assist you in your full-time staff appointment.

(*d*) Tax under Schedule D is normally assessed on a preceding-year basis and possibly nothing will have to be paid until you have been making weekly or monthly payments under Schedule E for a couple of years.

An author writing a book or newspaper articles on a freelance basis, however seldom, has a right to be assessed under Schedule D as a professional writer. If you yourself cannot persuade your tax inspector to adopt Schedule D, there is no choice but to employ an accountant—whose charges incidentally are themselves eligible as an expense under Schedule D.

There are, however, two kinds of Schedule D so far as authors are concerned. Those with a regular income from writing should be assessed under Case II of Schedule D of the Income Tax Act 1952. The net income *or loss* is the amount received less expenses wholly and exclusively incurred. If there is a net loss, it can be carried forward to the following year or set against other income in the same year, which may result in a rebate of tax paid on that other income. But where only very occasional and small payments are received, the isolated transactions may be assessed under Case VI of Schedule D of the Income Tax Act 1952; then a net loss cannot be offset against other income but only carried forward to be offset against any other income assessed under Case VI. The writer of a substantial book should not have undue trouble in persuading the inspector that Case II is the relevant one, for the writing of even a single book is more than a casual affair such as giving the odd lecture or undertaking the very occasional newspaper article.

The Accounting Period   The second essential point is that you should choose your accounting period or tax year sensibly at the start. Under Schedule D, your net income of your financial year, ending at any time prior to 5 April, is assessed in the following fiscal (tax) year. Thus if we call the first year A, and the second year B, your authorship income of year A will not be assessed until year B, and the rate of tax you pay will of course then depend on the combination of year A's authorship income and (presuming you are in a full-time job) year B's salary. Year A's tax liability under Schedule D will normally be paid in two instalments, on 1 January (toward the end of the tax year B) and on the following 1 July (in fact in tax year C).

The whole tax operation is governed by the fiscal year—that is the nation's financial year—ending on 5 April. You yourself, however, can adopt a different fiscal year and can usually postpone the payment of tax by making this end at a slightly later date, say at the end of April. The whole of the money you have earned as an author during the previous twelve months will thus not be assessed until the end of the nation's fiscal year, twelve months from the following 5 April. But you usually have only one chance to fix your personal accounting year, and once it has been fixed any change is likely to be expensive. The choice must be made carefully at the start, probably before you actually receive any income from your publisher. If you delay the appointment of an accountant to look after your tax affairs until you do receive royalties, at least make sure that you help him to help you by getting a Schedule D assessment based on your tax year ending at a date somewhat after 5 April, say 30 April.

Providing you can prove that you are writing with a view to earning income, and if you incur expenses well before any income arrives, you may be able to enjoy a honeymoon. The

method of working Schedule D normally results in the first
year's assessment being repeated automatically for two years
and if you chose your financial year wisely, for almost three
years. If your first assessment is a minus one you will be able
to set off this loss against other income arising in the nation's
fiscal year and will have a minus assessment for the next year
and also the one following if your own financial year ends after
5 April. It is therefore even more important that the first assessment should be a good one from your point of view. This is
usually possible if you get yourself classified as an author at the
earliest reasonable moment, which again probably means when
you start writing and can produce evidence that you aim to
write for profit and will be writing more than one book. It also
means that the greatest care should be taken to record expenses.
Note fully why you incurred what expenses on what project.
Thus 'Visit to Sahara Desert (to collect material for *Sahara
Lizard Life*—contract XYZ Publishers for publication 197?)'
is more convincing than a claim for mere 'Travel'.

WHAT EXPENSES QUALIFY?

Broadly you can claim any expenditure that has been wholly
and exclusively incurred in the pursuit of writing, with minor
exceptions such as that entertainment is now not an allowable
expense unless your guest should happen to be an overseas
buyer. The expenses need not be limited to any set proportion of
the income, or indeed have any relationship to the eventual income expected, there being no law to tell you that you must make
a profit out of your writing or other vocation. If you like to produce a painstaking piece of research at a high cost for a very
limited market and your expenses vastly outstrip the income,
that is your affair, though it would be only natural for the tax
inspector to scrutinise such accounts more closely than those
of a more profitable author and to question any marginal-
sounding items such as heavy travel and hotel bills.

It will, incidentally, be obvious that authors who write about places and things generally have stronger evidence of the need to run up an expense account than the novelist, playwright or poet who depends mainly on his imagination. It pays to keep a detailed record so that you do not forget items when you come to make up the account at the end of the year and can substantiate claims if there are arguments. Noting the expenditure in a diary and analysing it at the end is as convenient a method as any.

Travelling Expenses   These include the cost of travelling for research, to visit your publisher or a technical adviser or collaborator; and normally full hotel bills for yourself (but not for guests) and railway and other fares should be claimed. If you like to travel first class even if your book will not make a profit, that is your affair. But if you indulge in unnecessary and prolonged luxury at a resort, of course you cannot expect the taxman to accept that the expenditure was necessary. If the business of authorship takes you to Timbuctoo and while there you want an extra day for your own pleasure, admit the fact and deduct its cost from your bill. If you use your own car for business travel you should be able to charge in one of two ways. If the business mileage is fairly small, it will be simplest to charge a straight allowance of so much per mile—the same kind of rate that councils and companies pay their staff for using their personal cars for business purposes. If you make repeated journeys, however, you may want to charge the appropriate proportion of all your motoring expenses; for instance if the business use amounts to two-fifths of your total mileage, then you charge two-fifths of the depreciation of the capital cost of the car, the Road Fund licence, insurance, repairs, petrol and other costs.

Office costs   If you work at home on your book, even just occasionally, some household costs should be claimed: at least you will have used extra lighting and heating. Ideally you should have a separate work den and charge the appropriate proportion of all household expenses, including rates, repairs and decoration, cleaning, heating and so on. Thus if your study occupies one-eighth of the total area of the house, you charge one-eighth of the cost of external painting or of the fuel to run the central-heating system. But remember that the proportion of the house you claim for business purposes will probably be caught for capital gains tax when you come to sell the property at a profit: owner-occupied homes are of course normally exempt from the tax.*

The total cost of telephone calls (and of the telephone rental if business calls predominate), postages, stationery, files and photographic films should of course be claimed.

Maintenance of library   The initial creation of your library is technically a capital investment and does not qualify for tax relief, but its maintenance after it has been created is a running expenditure and eligible. The point is most simply illustrated by quoting the case of that essential annual reference work, *The Writers' and Artists' Year Book*. You should not claim relief on the purchase of the first year's edition you buy, which is a new capital asset. But you charge subsequent years' editions since these are replacements. But while a single reference work that comes out annually is a clear-cut example, it is not so easy to say just what constitutes the creation of a library and at what stage you start charging for additions on a maintenance basis. In practice, if you have a good nucleus of books and then charge a reasonable sum for 'maintaining library', even if in fact most of the new books are additions rather than replacements, you will generally be allowed the expense: in many cases, especially with technical books, you will anyway need to increase the size of the library to maintain its money value. But you cannot expect to be allowed the cost of first buying

* At the time of writing however it seems possible that capital gains tax will not be levied if no room has been *exclusively* used for business purposes, and it may therefore be better to admit some private use—in the study, for example, up to 10 per cent, claiming that it is 90 per cent for business.

a major set of books costing say £200. The cost of trade and technical journals is allowable.

Depreciation allowances These will almost certainly be given on capital items such as furniture or typewriters in your office. Tax relief may be obtained in one of two ways. You can either claim a depreciation allowance year by year on the cost of the original purchase, or you can accept the initial cost of supplying a capital item yourself without claiming any tax relief but then charge the whole of the cost of the eventual replacement.

The depreciation system is generally the more attractive. There is a scale of initial and annual allowances or percentages of the initial cost and carried-forward value that you can charge. You can include machines, furniture—including the office carpet and bookshelves on the wall—but not the house or any immovable part of it. The proportion of purchase price of the car used for business purposes can also be claimed this way.

The replacement basis is less satisfactory since it involves a long wait before you receive any tax relief at all. But authors who have begun by buying furniture and equipment without realising they can seek a depreciation allowance should therefore make sure that they enjoy a tax-free replacement in due course—though of course items like desks may never wear out.

A professional accountant is especially useful in checking that you claim all depreciation and replacement allowances possible—providing you keep a note of your purchases and report them to him.

Subscriptions Subscriptions to organisations and societies connected with or useful for your writing work are allowable, but the cost of attending the meetings and conferences of professional organisations does not always qualify. Press-cutting agency subscriptions of course qualify.

Secretarial help   If you employ an outside typist or secretary solely for work on your book, of course the expense should be charged in full.

Wife's or other relation's help   Authors are often helped by relations, most frequently male authors by their wives who may sometimes genuinely give up other possibilities of earning for this purpose. Work should be paid for even when done within the family, and substantial and genuine savings in tax can often be achieved. The wife is entitled to a separate set of allowances as a single person when working. If her husband is her sole employer, that means that the first part (at present almost £300) of her annual income will be totally exempt from tax while other substantial amounts will be taxed below the standard rate. And even if the wife does have another income (unearned income is deemed to be her husband's) the probability is that she is still earning less than her husband and therefore paying tax at a lower rate in the £. Generally the least tax is paid when the husband's and wife's earned incomes are equalised.

The wife must of course provide the services she is paid for, and the payments must actually be made, however the money is used thereafter. The wife may be paid for undertaking research in a library, for taking telephone calls and messages and making enquiries on the author's behalf, for reading and criticising the manuscript and retyping it, and even for the office proportion of cleaning the home if there is a separate office. What she is paid must be reasonable in relation to the services she performs, of course, but again it must be emphasised that an author is not compelled to make a profit from his writing, and providing his wife's services are essential they can be charged at the full current rates of pay for people doing such work even if the book will make a loss.

The wife is often deprived of her husband's company while he is writing a book, or the husband may feel neglected if the wife is the author, and joint participation in the project in some way or other may have constructive psychological as well as financial implications. It can be particularly fruitful if the non-author develops know-how that the author himself may lack: becoming, for instance, the photographer of the pair.

Payments to wives are most conveniently made on a fee basis for actual work performed. But regular and substantial payments may make it inevitable that she is classified as a regular employee of her husband, who then has to tax her income at source under Schedule E PAYE, which is a time-wasting nuisance apart from making it harder to claim expenses.

Insurance and pension   Make sure you insure your library and claim the cost of the policy. If you are dependent upon writing for your livelihood it is worth considering a policy guaranteeing you a certain minimum income in the event of disability. Whether your writing is a hobby or profession, life-insurance policies, especially when coupled with unit-trust schemes, are a useful means of accumulating capital while giving your family immediate insurance protection and saving tax. There are also useful tax-saving provisions for the self-employed person buying pension rights: at the time of writing up to 10 per cent of income can be diverted to pension policies.

Accountant's fees   As stressed earlier, if your affairs become in the least complicated, engage a professional accountant; his fee is an allowable expense against income.

A FEW OTHER TAX POINTS

Though it is generally only the writer of a best-seller who suffers from a sudden superfluity of income, paying much more tax than were the income more evenly spread over a longer period, all authors should be aware that 'spreading' provisions do exist. Briefly, no spreading of income is allowed if the book took twelve or fewer months to prepare and write. If it took between twelve and twenty-four months, one-half of lump-sum payments and of royalties received during the first two years following publication can be regarded as being earned in the year preceding that of receipt. If over twenty-four months were taken to produce the book, one-third of the income can be regarded as arising in each of the two years preceding receipt.

Since the earnings of most authors, from their regular jobs as well as from spare-time writing, will probably be rising year by year, the potential advantage of being able to transfer income backwards is obvious; but many factors, such as other income, changing personal allowances and the possibility of a drop in the standard rate of tax, have to be borne in mind.

A different kind of spreading provision is available for those who sell or lease their copyrights ten years or more after publication. The lump-sum income received does not have to be counted as all arising in one year, and may be spread forward over a maximum of six years. But you cannot take advantage of both this and the more usual spreading arrangement.

Incidentally, the outright sale of a copyright, even years after publication, does still constitute taxable income, at least if you live in the United Kingdom. If you are an accepted non-resident the income may be non-taxable—but if you are living abroad to save tax you will anyway need more professional guidance than can be given here.

If you sell work direct to a publisher or other customer in America, Canada, Australia, New Zealand and most European and a few other countries, you will be protected by the Double Taxation Agreement and not be taxed both in that country and in the United Kingdom—and the same applies if you are living abroad and earning money from a British publisher. A British publisher cannot however remit money overseas without first deducting tax at the standard rate unless the author provides the necessary certificate to enable him to do so—obtainable from the Inspector of Foreign Dividends, New Malden House, New Malden, Surrey.

DEATH DUTIES

Since copyright lasts fifty years beyond the author's death, it has to be taken into account for death-duty purposes. You can of course give your copyrights to your children before you die, but the usual death-duty provisions about gifts being brought back into your estate if they took place within a certain period before your death will apply. The valuation of copyrights on the death of an author is a delicate and technical matter, unfortunately not always fully understood by solicitors acting for the deceased's family. Low valuations are obviously desirable and in fact usually realistic, for whatever hope there may be of future income, rarely are there cast-iron guarantees of continuing sales and new printings.

9 The Book Business

BOOKS ARE DIFFERENT

ONE OF MY main aims in writing this work has been to brush aside some of the mystique that even today is summoned around anything to do with books and 'literature'. 'Of course, you are a *literary* man,' someone once told me, implying that someone on a higher plane should be excused some of the mundane considerations of life. Researching, writing, editing and publishing non-fiction is an everyday pursuit for many thousands of people, and as individuals we have no right to expect preferential consideration from the community.

But our products, as distinct from ourselves, do have some claim. 'Books are different' is a slogan successfully used by the Publishers Association and others for many years now as part of the campaign to ensure that the unique quality of books is appreciated, especially by the Government. The phrase first came into its own when a proposal to charge purchase tax on books was defeated, largely though the efforts of Sir Stanley Unwin, in the early days of the Second World War. More recently, books have been exempted from import restrictions and surcharges, and they are not directly taxed in any form. A tax on books, it is said, is a tax on learning, a tax on free communication and expression of opinion.

Books are different from the vast range of goods in the shops in combining a physical article with ideas. The physical product is only the container for wrapping up the information and the thoughts imparted by the author; yet it often has its own aesthetic appeal. A well-designed book would, for instance, be handled with care and interest by the foreigner with no understanding of English. Very few things combine a physical article with ideas. Films do, but then the film itself cannot be handled with joy; it can only be seen through a projector. Tape recordings and records also require intermediary equipment.

There is also the point that books are made to last. Not only are they often beautiful in themselves, so that it hurts to see them badly handled, but the reader usually takes care of them so that they continue to be capable of giving pleasure or providing information for many years to come. Those we buy today outlast ourselves, as many of those we inherited or buy second-hand outlived their original owners. Many children are first taught to take care of books when given a pictorial or story book once used by their parents or grandparents. At the extreme, rare books are among the safest investments, though their purchase solely for the financial motive by collectors who will never appreciate their intrinsic value is a negation of their real purpose.

Authors usually do their part in promoting interest in and understanding of books—the attitude that books are different. Many of us—and not only publishers—are ready to attack those who say that books are 'too expensive'. Why are they too expensive and compared with what? What else can give such immediate and yet such lasting satisfaction as a good book, purchased for perhaps the price of a meal for two or three in a reasonable restaurant, or for perhaps only half the cost of a single air ticket from London to Scotland?

THE NET BOOK AGREEMENT

The Net Book Agreement is of the greatest importance to non-fiction authors, for without it the economics of the British book trade would be radically changed, most of us believe for the worse. The agreement states simply that except for well-defined exceptions net books (virtually all but educational ones) may not be sold at less than the full published price. That the agreement has been upheld notwithstanding the general abolition of retail price maintenance demonstrates the strength of the 'books are different' campaign. Thus while multiple stores

I

cut the price of well-known brands of chocolate bars as 'loss leaders' to attract customers, they cannot offer the best-selling book of the day any more cheaply than does the specialist bookshop down the street. So most bestsellers continue to be bought through the specialist bookshops, which thus gain sufficient trade to enable them to carry a wide stock, including many titles that sell slowly and may remain on the shelves for months or even years.

If the agreement were abolished, total book sales would not necessarily drop. They could conceivably increase. But the cut-throat competition among stores offering the current bestsellers at lower prices would leave the stock-holding bookseller—who is to be found, if in a small way, in most British towns of 10,000 people or more—without his share of easy-selling lines. In the United States, where the book trade has no price-maintenance agreement, towns of up to 25,000 and even 50,000 people are without bookshops.

The difficulty is that we cannot have our cake and eat it. In accepting the protection that the agreement gives to books produced for minority audiences, we have to adhere to the rules even when they are inconvenient. This means that authors do not resell at less than the full published price any copies of their books bought from their publisher at trade terms. Copies can of course be given to friends and colleagues, but if they are sold it must be at full price (the author pocketing the retail profit). Maybe the Net Book Agreement will not collapse if an author quietly passes on three copies of his work to a sister or other close relation who asks for them, either to give away or to resell, but he should make sure that she in her turn will not sell them at less than full price. Apart from anything else, a book-seller who has taken the risk of investing in copies of a new book will hardly be encouraged to persist by hearing that one of his customers has 'got it more cheaply from the author's sister'.

Net books include virtually all new adult books apart from educational ones (on which booksellers can offer competitive discounts to attract institutional business). Libraries are normally entitled to buy net books at a discount of 10 per cent, but have to purchase them through bookshops or library suppliers holding a 'library licence'—an indication, perhaps, of just how seriously the agreement is treated by the Publishers and the Booksellers Associations. There are also one or two other licence schemes; for instance a businessman buying bulk copies of one book to give away as Christmas presents may obtain a small discount, providing the shop has specifically obtained permission for the transaction. Eventually bookshops holding surplus stock may of course sell it off cheaply, and a year or more after publication bookclubs may sell cheap editions to their members. Some 'simultaneous bookclubs' were formed recently, offering their members cheaper copies of books on first publication. Though many people in the trade dislike this infringement, the simultaneous clubs have been accepted within the framework of the Net Book Agreement on the understanding that publishers give advance warning of the titles involved so that booksellers can boycott them or keep down their orders.

ARE AUTHORS BADLY PAID?

The story that authors are among the most unfairly rewarded people in the community, that everyone from the publisher to the Chancellor of the Exchequer conspires to keep them down, is a well-worn thread in British folklore. Publishers grow rich while authors toil for the barest necessities of life; was it not once reported that the 'average earnings' of an author were only two or three hundred pounds a year, and how could anyone live on that? Then, how is it that the bookseller, who merely hands a copy of the book across the counter, makes three times as much on it as does the man who wrote it? And why should libraries be allowed to lend to dozens of readers a book on which only a single royalty is paid and which those people might otherwise have bought for themselves?

Personally I think most of this is nonsense, or at least that elements of grievance are exaggerated beyond reason by people who are, after all, professional communicators. I just do not accept that authors are on the whole badly treated. I did not accept it when I was an author, and I do not now that I am also a publisher. This, of course, is controversial; but consider:

Firstly, just who *are* 'authors'? My firm is not unusual among non-fiction publishers in that something like nine out of ten of its authors write in their spare time, as a supplementary activity, often on subjects arising out of their jobs and professions. Most would not wish to become full-time 'professional' authors, even if they trusted their own ability to produce a rapid succession of good books. Obviously the few most famous and successful writers in some fields will give up other employment—though even these people often combine writing with a little part-time lecturing or other paid occupation, if only to bring themselves into contact with the wide world—but the rest usually produce better books by not doing so. Starvation level threatens only those who, with inadequate talent, knowledge or self-discipline, have turned full-time authors for the prestige of it, or to be their own master—to be, at least in theory, free from a boss, from office hours, from daily travel, or whatever it is that they feel cramps their genius. If these writers do not earn enough, by and large the remedy is in their own hands. No one is compelled to become a full-time author; the fact that you have written one or two successful books does not justify the assumption that you can do nothing but writing in future; indeed, by renouncing another occupation you may be depriving yourself of a part of life that, for all its disadvantages, provided stimulation of a kind.

The 'average earnings' of authors are sometimes too readily quoted as though they should bear comparison with those of full-time professionals such as doctors. For instance, the Society of Authors can occasionally act as if it were a union for full-time employees, which does not make for better understanding of the books business as a whole. The Society, a non-profit making organisation which has done much valuable work for writers, gives advice, takes legal action on behalf of its members if it thinks that a publisher has unfairly broken an agreement, runs a pension scheme, publishes an enterprising magazine, *The Author*, and is responsible for certain prizes and awards to authors; but its tendency to regard authors as a distinct class set apart in the community can lead to naïvety when discussing their financial affairs.*

Second. Some authors complain that it is unfair that they receive only a single royalty when a copy of a book bought by a library is lent to many different readers over the years. For a long time there has been a campaign (backed by the Society of Authors) to establish some kind of public lending right to compensate the author and possibly also the publisher for the theoretical loss of sales and royalties. The individual book borrower, the library or the Government would pay a fee into a fund that would pay out compensation. Yet very many non-fiction titles could not be published at all without the support of public-library sales, which are easier to gauge and come earlier in the book's life than most other sales. Then, many books are bought privately for regular use or sheer joy of ownership after they have been seen or studied in libraries. It seems to me that generally it is only when a library strengthens the

---

* For instance, in 1966 the Society published a booklet by Richard Find-later called *The Book Writers: Who Are They?*, which discusses the results of an inquiry into authorship. On one page it states: 'By their own defini-tions just over half (56%) of the people who replied to the questionnaire were solely (46%) or principally (10%) occupied with authorship. These were the primaries.' But a few pages on we learn 'Taking the primary authors alone, only 35% obtained more than half their total livelihood from their books, and as many as 33% got less than a *tenth*—yet these are the authors who depend for a living on their writing.' Apart from the fact that anyone who obtains only a tenth of his income from one source can scarcely be said to be depending on that source for his livelihood, the self-classification of authors who opt to answer a questionnaire is obviously suspect. Indeed, elsewhere Mr Findlater states: 'Looked at as a whole, less than one third (31%) of all the primaries were authors both by activity and by writing income. This means that the majority depended for a living mainly or partially on another trade or profession, on a private income, or on other form of subsidy.' In other words even many of those classify-ing themselves as 'solely occupied with authorship' were in fact part-time writers with a full-time job.

binding, increasing the value of the physical book after the author has been paid royalties calculated on the original value, that there is any just complaint, and the cost of organising a supplementary royalty scheme for library usage would be needlessly wasteful. That greater support should be given to books is a quite different matter. The cuts in public-library spending in times of credit restriction hurt both writers and readers. Britain lags shockingly behind in the creation of a national library and in expenditure on school books. And there are other grievances that could usefully be removed—to quote one small example the six free copies of every title published that have to be given to copyright libraries including one in Eire.

Third. Some authors speak of bookshops as though they are parasites, fattening on proceeds which should go elsewhere. 'The bookshop gets 33⅓ per cent and I only get 10 per cent. Why?' The answer is in fact very simple. A one-third discount is common in the retail trade for articles similar to books in variety and price. Bookshops have heavy overheads including taxes, and not all the books they stock are eventually sold, while many others take a long time to find a customer. The economics of retail selling in fact mean that any lower discount would make business impossible; and as it is, many bookshops do not make enough profit to improve their premises and train fresh staff. Once you accept that the retailer needs one-third— and now there is a move to increase it to 35 per cent—it is obviously impossible that you as author should receive another third, leaving the publisher with only the remaining third out of which to pay all production bills, his staff and other overheads and interest charges, and make a profit. A 10 per cent stake in the total price—of which, remember, the publisher only receives two-thirds less the cost of carriage—is generally not unrealistic or unfair.

Fourth. If you read that your publisher has made a big profit, do not automatically assume it is at your expense. As in other industries, only the profitable firm succeeds, will be able to borrow money for future growth and to pay the tax bill, and will have guaranteed continuity. The author's worst fear should be of publishers that go bankrupt or sell out to larger firms who may lack any enthusiasm for the books taken over. It is bankruptcies and unsatisfactory takeovers and mergers that have really hurt many authors since the war. Profit too, is not always what it sounds. In the present year, out of every £10,000 profit, £4,500 has to be paid in Corporation Tax; the profit is in fact likely to be largely assessed on the value of stock not yet sold, but the tax collector of course demands cash and not books for settlement.

Fifth. Some authors say that it is not worth troubling to increase earnings since they are so heavily taxed. Unless your book sales are in the quarter-of-a-million bracket, this is not true. As was indicated in the last chapter, authors have many potential advantages from the tax point of view—if they are prepared to bother to exploit them or engage an accountant to do so. I duplicate this point here since it is so often the very people most bitter about the unprofitability of authorship who do not trouble to look after their financial matters properly. To shrug off such matters as beyond you or too much of a bore can only demonstrate to others that you are not truly competent over managing your affairs.

PUBLISHING AS A CAREER

Some readers of this book may be young people (possibly the children of authors) who have wondered about making publishing their career. For the right type of person, it can be among the most exciting of jobs, and today is by no means as badly paid as tradition has it, though it still calls for concentrated work over longer hours than are common in most other offices.

There is no specific pre-entry training course, and a degree or other qualification will not always gain priority, employers judging people very much for their practical ability to do the job. Basic literacy is obviously important, and flair and enthusiasm for books or for the subject matter covered may count for a lot, but just as important is the ability to grasp detail and work methodically, for publishing is a highly complex, detailed and fragmented business. Remember that very little actual research or writing is done in most publisher's offices, since most books have outside authors, and publishing is therefore not really an alternative to an academic post at a university. Otherwise the range of jobs is wide, and in most there are equal opportunities for men and women, though secretaries are normally female and representatives calling at bookshops and colleges male. In smaller firms responsibilities are often combined according to the talents available, a designer perhaps also doing estimating or production work, and an editor handling publicity; larger firms tend to work in watertight compartments. A smaller firm should therefore be more attractive to someone seeking an insight into publishing as a whole. Most small firms are quick to recognise and use talent, and switching to another job within the firm is often simple enough.

The problem, especially in small firms, is matching the supply and demand. Most publishers are inundated with enquiries from would-be employees, especially on the editorial side, but often still find it difficult to obtain the right people. Few publishers have more than one or two openings of the same kind at any time, and there are sharp differences in the requirements of different firms even for nominally-similar jobs. Girls have a big advantage in making an initial entry because there is always a shortage of good shorthand secretaries. The girl determined to make publishing her career should take a crash secretarial course even if she has a degree. Her first job might be mundane, but once inside a publisher's office she will quickly have an opportunity to prove herself—while shorthand has its uses even in non-secretarial jobs. Many publishing jobs are advertised in the weekly trade paper, *The Bookseller*, though so many school and university leavers proffer their services that it is often not necessary to advertise for junior staff. He who shouts first and loudest tends to be heard most. Write in detail giving your reasons for wanting to go into publishing, to a firm of your choice, or to several firms, some months before you will be free to take a job, and offer yourself for interview. If you do not hear, send a reminder six or eight weeks later. Publishing is a branch of the communications business, and the prospective boss takes note of those who can successfully communicate their enthusiasm.

10 The Author's Library and Source Material

YOUR OWN LIBRARY

THE CENTREPIECE of the author's own reference library should be an encyclopaedia, ideally perhaps *The Encyclopaedia Britannica*, though even the smallest 'complete' encyclopaedia, *Everyman's*, is useful, despite its lack of an index and its sometimes outdated bibliographical references. The one-volume encyclopaedias, as and when you can afford them, are not to be despised. A good dictionary is of course essential, and most people's choice will be *The Concise Oxford Dictionary*, though the longer, two-volume *Shorter Oxford Dictionary* may repay the extra cost and shelf room.

Most people writing the kind of book with which this volume deals will need a good atlas and gazetteer, if only to check exactly where a place is, how the name is spelt, or how far it lies from the next big town. The atlas volume is a substantial bonus for buyers of *The Encyclopaedia Britannica*; more detailed is *The Times Atlas*. *Webster's Geographical Dictionary*, listing over 40,000 geographical names with concise notes, solves many problems, but because of its worldwide coverage cannot include most of the smallest places. The AA *Road Books* list many British villages as well as towns, and even the AA *Members' Handbook* is a useful reference tool, quoting distances between towns and population figures as well as including a brief atlas section. *Bartholomew's Gazetteer* of the British Isles is invaluable and also *Bartholomew's Survey Atlas of England and Wales*.

The traditional authority on points of English is H. W.

Fowler's *A Dictionary of Modern English Usage*, and the same author's *The King's English* and *Modern English Usage* remain actively in circulation though no longer modern. G. H. Vallins has more recently added *Good English, Better English* and *Best English*, normally available in both hardback and paperback form, as is E. Partridge's *Usage and Abusage*. For the technical man turning to writing for the first time, J. Mitchell's *A First Course in Technical Writing* can be recommended.

The Oxford Companion to English Literature remains an invaluable reference work for many authors, and *Brewer's Dictionary of Phrase and Fable* is another famous standby. Roget's *Thesaurus* and other dictionaries of synonyms occasionally spur the mind but many authors find them not quite so useful as expected. The library should however include a good dictionary of quotations, such as a modern edition of *Bartlett's Familiar Quotations* or *The Oxford Dictionary of Quotations*.

A few other general reference works (to supplement books on his own subject) will ensure that the author can answer at least a reasonable proportion of his own queries quickly. There should be one standard history of Europe or England, a dictionary of dates (*Everyman's Dictionary of Dates* is good value), a classical dictionary, a technical and/or scientific dictionary, and of course *Whitaker's Almanac*, a mass of up-to-date information on innumerable topics; it is worth buying afresh each year. So is that essential reference tool especially designed for the freelance writer, *The Writers' and Artists' Year Book*. Its range of information has increased steadily over the years. It lists not only British and foreign publications and publishers with their likely requirements, but literary agencies, typing services, press-cutting agencies, literary prizes and awards, societies of interest to authors and journalists, and much more; it also includes up-to-date sections on subjects such as libel, and the author and national insurance.

The Statesman's Year Book is a useful annual for anyone concerned with trade statistics and other details from all the countries of the world; but the individual author cannot expect to keep up-to-date copies of all the expensive and useful annuals available, ranging from *Who's Who* to *The Stock Exchange Year Book*, and should concentrate on those particularly relevant to his interests, turning to the local reference library for the others.

Recent years have seen the publication of a growing number of specialised dictionaries and handbooks of varying quality, and indeed the literature of many subjects, technical and other, is expanding so rapidly that it is worth making a point of borrowing or studying the newest additions in your local or institutional library, to assess their worth and to study their bibliographies. For instance, few of the numerous books published on local history during the past fifteen years are mentioned in standard encyclopaedias or other reference works, and even the *Local History* volume in the 'Teach Yourself' series was published before the subject had its great awakening at the end of the 1950s and in the 1960s. J. P. M. Pannell's *Techniques of Industrial Archaeology* is the kind of work especially valuable for its bibliography.

Such bibliographies of course list the traditional source books as well as newer titles, and once owning a working library of, say, an encyclopaedia, twenty general and perhaps another twenty or thirty specialist books currently in print, an author will often be wise to go back to some of the earlier works long since available only secondhand. So far as money and space permit, most of us find that even second-rate reference books can come into their own, supplementing a more standard work.

Local historians and topographical writers will find books published a century or more ago especially valuable. Moreover, early travel, technical and other works have a charm of their own and may prove excellent investments if properly stored. Little has been published this century to match the quality of the Murray *Handbooks* and the directories and gazetteers of William White and others (now being reprinted); in fact the only major postwar contribution of any permanence in this field is the Pevsner *Buildings of England* series, uneven in its treatment and quality, but of high average achievement.

To keep abreast of useful literature, old and new, visits to libraries and antiquarian booksellers are obviously called for, and you can join the mailing lists of antiquarian booksellers specialising in your field. But today there is a seller's market for standard source material, and when a catalogue arrives it needs studying quickly: often orders should be sent by telegram or telephone. Remember that it is worth paying a lot more for a reference tool which has remained in demand for generations and whose price is likely to continue rising than it is for an ephemeral work of more doubtful quality. Good, scarce works will continue to appreciate—even if for argument's sake they are reprinted. Much primary source material is now being reprinted, of course, and if interested you can get your name added to the mailing lists of publishers producing substantial lists, such as Frank Cass, David & Charles, and Dawsons.

USE OF OTHER LIBRARIES

Public libraries perform two main functions. They lend a wide range of books for the reader to use at home; and they keep another range to be consulted in their own buildings. Many authors make surprisingly little use of both services and indeed fail to understand just what facilities are at their command.

The local branch of your public-library authority of course has a lending department, from which any resident can select books either for study or for light reading. But that is only the tip of the iceberg. The librarian will also be pleased to obtain any work you need for study purposes that is available for loan at a library anywhere in the country.

You need not even visit the local library; as this is a postal service, it is sometimes quicker to write direct to the headquarters of your library service (the city library in a city, the headquarters of the county library, probably in the county town, if you live outside a city) stating what you wish to borrow; give all particulars you know if the book is old and obscure. You can request almost any non-fiction work, but not novels unless you need something for study or research. There may be some delay on titles only just published.

If the book required is in stock, your library (or its headquarters library) will of course supply it immediately. If there is no copy at headquarters but one at a branch library, the branch will be asked to send it direct to you. If your city or county library has no copy anywhere, the request will be passed to the regional library loan scheme, and the book may come from any branch of any library authority within your region. Failing that, the request will be passed on again so that ultimately the lending resources of the whole of Great Britain will be at your disposal; the National Central Library acts as clearinghouse for loans and maintains a union catalogue of nonfiction books in all co-operating libraries which include unversity, college and commercial libraries as well as virtually all public libraries. And all you have to do is acknowledge receipt of the book if requested to do so, and normally return it at the end of a month, paying only the cost of return postage. It is genuinely a bargain—so much so that some otherwise well-informed people find it hard to believe. It is a service especially for those engaged in research and study and should not be used frivolously, though if you really need them there is no reason why you should not request several books together, and an extension for a second or third month's loan will be granted, unless other borrowers are wanting the book.

Some expensive reference works and most very rare books of course do not leave library premises. An expensive annual stocked by the larger libraries which has special value to authors is *British Books in Print*. It contains both author and title indexes, so that you can check whether any other books are available with titles similar to the one you have dreamed up— indeed that your proposed title has not already been used— and can see if a book published years ago is still in print. A comparable list of American books should also be found in the largest libraries. Big libraries will also have *The Dictionary of National Biography*, a run of *Who Was Who* as well as the current *Who's Who*, *Keesing's Contemporary Archives*—an invaluable record of current events at home and abroad kept continuously up-to-date—and back as well as current issues of standard reference works such as *Jane's Fighting Ships* and Census and other Government reports. There may be old newspaper files (sometimes also available for consultation at the office of the newspaper or its successor), runs of magazines old or new, maps (which can prove especially useful to local, industrial and transport historians), and collections of photographs. The best libraries may have some kind of index to their collections of printed and photographic material of local interest, and will also act as signpost to the local record office. Most counties now have established record offices and many have built up substantial collections of documents and records.

To some extent your local library should also be able to act as signpost to the greater resources of the national institutions, such as the Public Record Office or the Kensington Science Museum or the National Maritime Museum at Greenwich, which not only have substantial collections of their own but will often give guidance to the *bona fide* author. It is usually better to write in advance, stating what you want and why, rather than to call without warning and have your enquiry handled by whoever happens to be on duty. It is always worth emphasising that you are writing a book and mentioning the publisher if that has been fixed; most libraries and institutions are worried by a stream of less serious enquirers wanting information to settle bets or to produce school essays. Even the busiest administrators have time to spare to guide the author who seeks specific guidance, as opposed to schoolgirls who write asking for 'all you know' on a wide subject.

The British Museum, with its main Reading Room, its Newspaper Library, Map Room, State Paper Room and many specialist services, is for serious enquirers prepared to complete the formalities and with a fair amount of time at their disposal. A series of leaflets describing the facilities and the formalities is available on request. Except by special order from the Trustees, admission is only for those over 21 and a ticket must be obtained. 'Applications should be accompanied by a written recommendation from a person of recognised position based upon *personal* knowledge and certifying that he or she is a fit and proper person to use the Reading Room.'

KEEPING ABREAST OF YOUR SUBJECT

The increase in the number of books published of the kind considered in this work alone demonstrates how rapidly many subjects are changing—and not only the highly technical fields. New areas of study like industrial archaeology are being developed fast; many semi-technical books quickly become obsolete and two more specialist titles replace a single older one. The study of almost all aspects of both arts and sciences is becoming more detailed.

The successful author must keep abreast of the changes, which above all means knowing just what other books and papers on his subject have been published. The obvious course is to subscribe to the specialist magazines, to run through the back numbers and to join any appropriate organisations in order to receive their journals or other publications even if not actively to take part in meetings and courses. Note what second-hand booksellers, publishers and other suppliers advertise in the magazines and journals. You may be lucky enough to have a bookseller who will keep you informed of new titles appearing on your subject; indeed some authors deliberately obtain their new books by post from one of the top dozen or so academic booksellers in order to receive catalogues listing new titles and prospectuses of new series.

The Times Literary Supplement can be a useful investment for the author wanting to keep abreast of the publishing and literary scene as a whole. Only a few books of the kind dealt with here receive long reviews in the body of the paper, but many more are given short notices in the 'Books Received' section, and most titles are advertised by their publishers. For those more interested in the trade, *The Bookseller* lists all new books published each week (or, in the last issue of the month, during each month), and again contains many publishers' advertisements. The two Export Numbers list virtually all books to be published during the following six months. Few magazines now give a complete review coverage of all books published in their fields, and while the learned journals tend to review a greater range of titles their notices often appear too late to be useful. The popular press, including the Sunday 'quality' papers, review only a small selection of books in total and only a small proportion of these are definitive non-fiction.

Many authors lose interest in a subject after publishing a book on it. The trouble comes when the first edition sells out and the publisher asks if there are any revisions for a reprint. Even if your main interest changes, if you would like your book to be reprinted (however unlikely that might appear when you receive your first royalty statement) do something to keep abreast of changes, if only by noting down the titles of books and papers that must be consulted.

STORING YOUR MATERIAL

The best books are often those based on material collected over a long period—material gleaned from other books, from original records, newspaper cuttings, magazine files, interviews with old people, and often from many other sources as well. It is all too easy for the part-time author to be so swamped by paper by the time he comes to start writing that he wastes valuable energy looking for what should be handy—or finds he has no identification details of a paper he once read and must consult.

Introduce a simple filing and recording system. Everyone has his own method, and the best are not elaborate, but do something to prevent waste and muddle. A simple card index listing where main references to topics may be found (in books, newspaper cuttings, transcriptions of notes and the like) can be useful. A cunningly simple device is a photocopy of the index of the principal existing work on the subject with wide margins in which you can indicate the whereabouts of the notes and other material you hold. Newspaper cuttings are a particular curse if not stuck in a scrap book or properly filed—and the paragraph in today's paper which you stow away carefully could solve an otherwise elusive problem when you come to write in eighteen months' time. The most recent developments and problems can sometimes prove the hardest to unravel, simply because they have not had time to be documented.

Acknowledgments

FIRSTLY, acknowledgments to two publishers and writers of the old school who gave me early interest and enthusiasm. One is the late Sir Stanley Unwin, whose *Truth About Publishing* remains one of the few great books on the industry. I imbibed it many years ago, and though I deliberately refrained from consulting it at any stage of the creation and execution of this work, its influence is obvious. The second is my father, Gilbert Thomas, as it happens a friend of Sir Stanley, who published much of his work; long before I reached literacy my father's postbag was a source of delight, and though our types of writing and publishing are opposite, much of the experience and the spirit is shared.

A book I have found particularly stimulating and should like warmly to recommend is G. R. Elton's *The Practice of History*. This takes the view that it is important to publish history, to *communicate* the results of research, even if this entails taking a chance that something here and there may not be wholly and finally correct. Much advice is given to help the lay historian bring a professional touch to his task; it is emphasised for instance that amateurs who have not read widely enough can too often look foolish by expressing amazement at a local discovery of something that was in fact commonplace. There are sections on 'Purpose', 'Research', 'Writing' and 'Teaching'.

Everyone who has extended my publishing experience has in a sense contributed to this book, and I have had many individuals in mind while writing it—including the chap who said he could not post his manuscript since I would not understand it unless he was there to explain it personally. My thanks are sincere to all those who (usually more constructively than the chosen example) have unconsciously helped. Especial thanks are of course due to those members of my staff, and to printers and others, who have given specific advice on the handling of certain topics. On financial matters I am particularly indebted to K. G. Davis FCA. For comments on the common-sense approach to production matters, thanks are due to Mrs Pam Darlaston, in charge of our firm's letterpress production department.

Convention rules that one should thank one's wife. The problem is how to phrase thanks to Pamela in a way that does not seem merely the fulfilment of convention. We first met in a reference library and ever since have had a close working partnership. As our firm's editorial director, she has helped shape the basic philosophy and ways of working which find their place in this book, and of course has given much advice on this specific project. It is indeed virtually a work of joint authorship.

Then I should like to return to *The Writers' and Artists' Year Book*: were there not so excellent a reference book on the market, I should have succumbed to the temptation of including more material (such as on copyright and libel) that might quickly have become dated. Since the reference job is done so well, I have been left free to deal with the broader issues.

Finally, acknowledgments are due to the Publishers Association and to the British Federation of Master Printers for permission to reproduce material in the appendices.

Appendix 1

SPECIMEN CONTRACT

THE PUBLISHERS ASSOCIATION recently produced a specimen contract and explanatory notes for the guidance of their members. Both documents are reproduced here by special permission. It should be remembered that contracts vary sharply according to the type of publishing (for instance most contracts for educational books will not go to such detail concerning subsidiary rights) while most publishers will anyway be using their own individual form of contract pre-dating the circulation of this specimen. The notes were designed solely for the guidance of publishers but are included here since they reveal certain points likely to interest authors.

MEMORANDUM OF AGREEMENT made this
day of   19   BETWEEN   of
                (hereinafter called "the Author", which expression shall where the context admits include the Author's executors, administrators and assigns) of the one part and
of
(hereinafter called "the Publisher", which expression shall where the context admits include the Publisher's executors, and assigns, or successors in business, as the case may be) of the other part WHEREBY it is mutually agreed between the parties hereto as follows:

1. The Author agrees to write/has written a work at present entitled
(hereinafter referred to as "the work") consisting of
                words.

2. The Author undertakes to deliver/has delivered two copies of the complete typescript of the work ready for the printer by
    Should the Author neglect to deliver the typescript by the prescribed date the Publisher may, if he thinks fit, decline to publish the work, in which case this Agreement shall be terminated subject to the proviso that the Author shall not be at liberty to publish

the work elsewhere without first offering it to the Publisher on the terms of this Agreement.

The Publisher shall not be responsible for any accidental loss or damage to the work, including illustrations and other material, by fire or otherwise, while it is in his custody or in the course of production.

3. If, in the opinion of the Author and Publisher, illustrations, maps or diagrams are considered necessary, material suitable for reproduction shall be supplied by the Author at the Author's own cost at the same time as the typescript is delivered. The Author shall at his own expense obtain from the owners of any material in the work of which the copyright is not his own written permission for the use of such material.

If in the opinion of the Publisher an index is required it shall be supplied by the Author or at the Author's expense within of receipt of the final paged proofs.

4. The Author undertakes to read and check proofs of the work and to return them to the Publisher within days of their receipt and to bear the amount, if any, by which the cost of the Author's alterations, other than printer's errors, exceeds per cent. of the cost of composition.

5. The Author hereby warrants to the Publisher and his assigns and licensees that the said work is an original work, has not been published in volume form within the territories covered by this Agreement and is in no way whatever a violation of any existing copyright, that it contains nothing libellous, that all statements contained therein purporting to be facts are to the best of the Author's knowledge and belief true, that the Author has full power to make this Agreement and will indemnify the Publisher against any loss, injury or damage (including any legal costs or expenses and any compensation costs and disbursements paid by the Publisher on the advice of Counsel to compromise or settle any claim) occasioned to the Publisher in consequence of any breach of this warranty.

The Author further warrants that the said work contains no defamatory, obscene or improper material.

6. The Publisher shall, unless prevented by war, strikes, lock-outs, or other circumstances beyond his control, produce and publish the work at his own risk and expense with reasonable promptitude. The Publisher shall have the entire control of the publication; and

the paper, printing, binding, jacket and embellishments, the manner and extent of advertisement, the number and distribution of free copies for the Press or otherwise and the price and terms of sale of the first or any subsequent edition, shall be in his sole discretion.

7. The published price of the work shall be about   per copy in the first instance, but the Publisher shall have power in his discretion from time to time to alter the published price.

8. In consideration of the payments hereinafter mentioned the Author hereby grants to the Publisher the sole and exclusive right to produce and publish the work or any abridgement of the work or any substantial part of the work in volume form for the legal term of copyright throughout the world, and undertakes that he will not during the continuance of this Agreement without the consent of the Publisher prepare otherwise than for the Publisher any work which shall be an expansion or abridgement of the said work or of a nature likely to affect prejudicially the sales of the said work.

9. The Publisher agrees to pay the Author the following royalties or fees in respect of volume or sheet sales of the work in the English language during the legal term of copyright:

(a) On the British published price of all copies sold, excluding such copies as may by subsequent clauses of this Agreement, or as may otherwise be mutually agreed, be sold subject to a different royalty: per cent.

(b) On copies sold at special terms for export or at a discount of fifty per cent. or more, except as provided in sub-clause (c):   per cent. of the net amounts received by the Publisher

(c) On copies of any edition or editions of the work, whether specially printed or not and whether bound or in sheets, sold for publication or distribution in the U.S.A. or elsewhere overseas: per cent. of the Publisher's net receipts, unless such copies are sold subject to a royalty on the published price in which case sub-clause (d) or (h) shall apply

(d) On all fees or royalties received by the Publisher on account of an edition or editions of the work published in the U.S.A.:   per cent. of the Publisher's net receipts

(e) On all copies sold of any cheaper edition or editions of the

work, other than in paperback, issued by the Publisher at two thirds or less of the original published price:
per cent. of such published price, provided that on copies sold at special terms for export or at a discount of fifty per cent. or more the royalty shall be   per cent. of the Publisher's net receipts from such sales

(f) On all copies sold of any paperback edition of the work issued by the Publisher under his own imprint the royalty shall be   per cent., except that on copies sold at special terms for export or at a discount of fifty per cent. or more the royalty shall be   per cent. of the Publisher's net receipts from such sales

(g) On all royalties received by the Publisher on account of an edition or editions of the work printed in paperback by other parties under licence from the Publisher for sale within the territories covered by this Agreement (other than the U.S.A.):   per cent. of the Publisher's receipts

(h) On all royalties received by the Publisher on account of an edition published in the English language on the Continent of Europe or elsewhere overseas (other than the U.S.A.) under licence from the Publisher: per cent. of the Publisher's net receipts

(i) On all royalties received by the Publisher on account of any book club or any other edition published in the English language for sale within the territories covered by this Agreement (other than the U.S.A.) under licence from the Publisher: per cent. of the Publisher's net receipts

The royalties on sales under (a) and (b) shall be   per cent. of the royalties specified if by mutual agreement, in order to keep the book in print and circulation as long as possible, the Publisher undertakes a small reprint of   copies or less.

10. No royalties shall be paid in respect of the following:

(a) Copies of the work presented to the Author, or to others, or to the Press;

(b) copies of the work destroyed by fire, water, enemy action, in transit, or otherwise;

(c) copies of the work sold at or below cost of production.

11. In consideration of the payment by the Publisher to the Author of the following percentages of all moneys received by him in

respect of the under-mentioned rights the Author hereby grants the said rights in so far as they are not granted by clause 8 above to the Publisher within the territory specified in that clause during the term of this Agreement:

(a) The right to reproduce extracts from the work in books, periodicals and elsewhere, including any maps, plans or other illustrations provided by the Author: per cent.

(b) Digest rights (i.e. the right to publish an abridgement of the work in a single issue of a periodical or newspaper) and book condensation rights (i.e. the right to publish a shortened form of the work in volume form): per cent.

(c) Second and subsequent serial rights (i.e. the right to publish extracts from the work in successive issues of a periodical or newspaper following publication of the work in volume form): per cent.

(d) Single issue rights (sometimes known as "one-shot" periodical or newspaper rights) i.e. the right to publish the complete work in a single issue of a periodical or newspaper: per cent.

(e) The right to produce or reproduce the work or any part thereof by film micrography, Xerography or by gramophone records or by the means of any other contrivance whether by sight or sound or a combination of both, except in so far as reproduction is for use as part of or in conjunction with a commercial cinematograph film: per cent.

(f) Strip Cartoon rights (sometimes called Picturization Book rights): per cent.

(g) Translation Rights: per cent.

12. The sale of the following rights shall be negotiated on behalf of the Author by the Publisher who shall retain the following percentages of the net amounts received in payment for such rights:

(a) First Serial rights (i.e. the right to publish extracts from the work in successive issues of a periodical or newspaper prior to publication in volume form): per cent.

(b) Dramatic and Film rights: per cent.

(c) Television Broadcasting rights: per cent.

(d) Sound Broadcasting rights per cent.

13. (*a*) The net proceeds from any claim in respect of infringement of the copyright of the work shall be divided equally between the Author and the Publisher.

(*b*) In respect of any net payment received for the use of the work in any country not a signatory of the Berne Union or the Universal Copyright Convention, the Author and the Publisher shall share in proportion of eighty-five per cent. to the Author and fifteen per cent. to the Publisher.

14. The Author shall be entitled to receive on publication six presentation copies of the first edition of the work, and shall have the right to purchase on trade terms further copies for personal use but not for resale.

15. The Publisher shall render the first two accounts of the said work as at   and   next following the date of first publication and subsequently annually as at and all moneys due to the Author shall be paid to him within three months of the said accountancy dates provided, however, that no accounts need be submitted unless specifically demanded nor payment made in respect of any year in which the sum due is less than £   in which case the amount will be carried forward to the next accountancy date.

16. To keep the work up-to-date the Author, if called upon by the Publisher, shall without charge to the Publisher edit and revise all editions of the work during the currency of this Agreement and shall supply any new matter that may be necessary to that end. In the event of the Author neglecting or being unable by reason of death or otherwise to edit or revise the work, or supply new matter where needed, the Publisher may engage some other person to edit or revise the work, or supply new matter, and may deduct the expense thereof from payments due to the Author under this Agreement.

17. The Publisher shall not less than two years after first publication be entitled to sell any surplus stock as a remainder at the best price such remainder stock will fetch. If that price is more than the cost of production, the Publisher shall pay the Author ten per cent. of the amount realized by such sale, and this shall be in lieu of other royalties.

18. If the work shall become out of print and not be available in any edition issued by the Publisher or authorized by him the Author

may give   months' notice in writing to the Publisher
to re-issue or reprint the work. In the event of the Publisher's failure to comply with such notice other than through circumstances
beyond his control all the Publisher's rights in the work (but not
those deriving from the option in clause 20 hereof) shall upon
expiration of the said notice determine without prejudice to all
rights of the Publisher and any third party in respect of any agreement properly entered into by the Publisher hereunder with any
such party.

19. If the Publisher at any time by himself or anyone acting on his
behalf wilfully fails to fulfil or comply with any of the conditions
accepted by him in this Agreement within one month after written
notification from the Author of such failure, or should the Publisher go into liquidation, other than voluntary liquidation for purposes of reconstruction, this Agreement shall thereupon determine
and the Author shall be free to license any other person to print
and publish the work, notwithstanding anything to the contrary
contained or implied in any part of this Agreement but without
prejudice to all rights of the Publisher and any third party in respect
of any agreement properly entered into by the Publisher hereunder
with any such party.

20. It is hereby agreed that the Publisher shall have the first refusal
(including the first opportunity to read and consider for publication) of the Author's next   works suitable for publication in volume form, and the Author shall offer the Publisher for
this purpose the same rights and territories as those covered by this
Agreement. Such book or books shall each be the subject of a fresh
agreement between the Author and the Publisher, on terms which
shall be fair and reasonable.

The Publisher shall exercise this option within   of
receipt of the complete typescript or copy, except that he shall not
be required to exercise it until two months after the publication of
the book which is the subject of this Agreement.

21. If any difference shall arise between the Author and the Publisher touching the meaning of this Agreement or the rights and the
liabilities of the parties thereto, the same shall be referred to the
arbitration of two persons (one to be named by each party) or their
mutually agreed umpire, in accordance with the provision of the
Arbitration Act, 1950, or any amending or substituted statute for
the time being in force.

SPECIMEN CONTRACT—NOTES
(Based upon the "Guide to Royalty Agreements")

General   The percentages indicated in these Notes are merely illustrations. Each publisher will naturally decide his own in relation to his own circumstances and general practice.

If it is desired to add riders to individual clauses and there is not space for their insertion in the printed standard form of contract, they may be added at the end, prefaced by "Rider to Clause 5" etc.

Clause 1   The words "to write" or "has written" to be deleted as appropriate.

The length of the work is generally expressed as "some [80,000] words", about [60,000] words", "not less than. . . .", not more than. . . .", etc.

Clause 2   The words "two copies of" may be deleted from the first line if only one copy is required. A second copy of the typescript may be useful (a) for the jacket artist. (b) for use in selling serial rights or placing the book in other markets.

An agreed date to be inserted at the end of the first paragraph.

If an advance payment is to be made in respect of an uncompleted work on signature of the contract (see note on Clause 8(a), below), it may be desirable to add the following words at the end of the second paragraph: "and subject also to the proviso that the Author shall refund to the Publisher any advance payment made by him to the Author under this Agreement."

Clause 3   Some publishers leave the decision as to whether there shall be an index (see the second paragraph) to be based on "the opinion of the *Author and* the Publisher", and the italicized words may be inserted if required. On the other hand, it needs to be borne in mind that not all authors are necessarily good judges of the way their work may be used, and that it is the Publisher and not the Author who is likely to be criticized in reviews if a necessary index is omitted.

A suitable period, depending on the complexity of the

work, needs to be inserted in the second paragraph. If the work requires no index (as in the case of a novel) the whole paragraph should be deleted.

Clause 4 The period commonly allowed for the Author's checking of proofs is *fourteen* days, but a longer period may be required for a complex work. The shorter period allows a reminder to be sent.

The Author is generally expected to bear the cost of his alterations if they exceed ten per cent. of the cost of composition.

Clause 5 Some publishers extend the first paragraph of this clause by adding after "warranty" the words: "or arising out of any claim alleging that the work constitutes an infringement of copyright or contains libellous or defamatory matter." (See Note (ii) on p.8 of the Guide to Royalty Agreements.)

Some publishers also add the following paragraph to this clause: "The first decision as to whether to contest any claim or to seek to compromise or settle any claim shall rest with the Publisher, subject to the proviso that should such a decision be made without the Author's consent the Publisher shall have no claim against the Author."

Such a rider can be useful if there is any danger that the Author might, through inadequate understanding of the workings of the law, insist that a claim be contested when prudence would dictate otherwise.

Some publishers, when sub-licensing a paperback edition customarily ask the Author to give a separate indemnity to the paperback house.

Clause 8 This clause secures all volume rights in any language throughout the world. If only English language rights or specified territorial rights are to be acquired the clause will need to be altered accordingly. No other consequential changes are needed in this standard form of contract.

Clause 8 *(a)* If it is desired to make the Author an advance payment, the following clause (adapted as necessary) may be inserted in the space after clause 8:

"The Publisher agrees to pay to the Author in advance and on account of all sums that may become due to the Author under this Agreement the sum of .... Pounds payable [as to fifty per cent. on signature of this Agreement and fifty per cent.] on publication of the work."

This clause is not printed in the standard agreement because advance payments are not made in respect of all kinds of books. A deleted advance payment clause may give the Author the impression that advance payments are invariably made whereas an inserted one will show that they are not.

If a clause is suggested to the Publisher specifying that an advance shall be "in respect of all *the above* sums" etc., particular care needs to be exercised as to where the clause is inserted.

Clause 9 (a) The Publisher may desire to extend this sub-clause by a scale of royalties, generally rising by steps of two and a half per cent., e.g.: "[ten] per cent. on the first [3,000] copies sold, [twelve and a half] per cent. on the next [5,000] copies sold", etc.

(b) The expressions "special terms for export" and "at a discount of fifty per cent. or more" are not alternatives but complementary, the latter not necessarily referring to export sales but to large bulk sales at special terms. The royalty is usually ten per cent. of the amounts received.

Some publishers of general books and fiction sometimes agree a rising scale of royalties on such sales, related to the published price rather than to the amounts received. Such a scale usually starts at a royalty half that of the commencing home royalty and rises more slowly, e.g.: "[five] per cent. on the first [3,000] copies sold, [six] per cent. on the next [5,000] copies sold", etc.

(c) The royalty here is commonly ten and sometimes twelve and a half per cent.

(d) The payment to the Author under this sub-clause is commonly seventy-five per cent.

(e) The common royalties in this sub-clause are ten per cent. on the published price, and ten per cent. of net receipts, respectively.

(f) The royalty here is generally seven and a half per cent. in both cases.

(g) The Author's normal share of paperback royalties is fifty per cent., but may be fifty-five per cent. where the paperback royalty is ten per cent., or sixty per cent. where it is twelve and a half per cent. or more or where the advance payment for paperback rights exceeds the aggregate royalty that would accrue from the sale of 100,000 copies.

(h) The royalty is normally fifty per cent. of receipts.

(i) The royalty is normally fifty per cent. of receipts. The tailpiece to this clause may be expressed in more general terms if desired, e.g.: "The royalties . . . shall be subject to a reduction by mutual agreement if . . . the Publisher undertakes a small reprint which he could not, by reason of its size and the prevailing cost of manufacture, undertake on the above royalty terms." It is probably wiser, however, to be specific.

[Seventy-five] per cent. of the normal royalties on re-prints of [1,500] copies or less would probably be normal in present circumstances.

Clause 10   Sub-Clause (c) needs to be read in conjunction with Clause 16, dealing with remainders.

Clause 11   (a) Fifty per cent. is normal.
(b) Fifty per cent. is normal.
(c) Seventy-five per cent. is normal.
(d) Fifty per cent. is normal.
(e) Fifty per cent. is common.
(f) Fifty per cent. is normal.
(g) This may vary from ninety per cent. to seventy-five per cent., according to the publisher's costs (e.g. acting as or employing an agent).

Clause 12   (a) Ten per cent. is normally the Publisher's share.
(b) Ten per cent. is normal.
(c) Twenty-five per cent. is normally expected by the Publisher.
(d) Twenty-five per cent. is normal.

Clause 13
(a) and (b)   No comment required.

Clause 14 No comment required.

Clause 15 The Publisher's normal accounting dates to be inserted. Accounts are not normally rendered nor payments made where the sum due is less than £5.

Clause 16 A more complex clause is needed to provide for the revision of technical and other specialized works likely to enjoy a prolonged demand. An example of such a clause is given on pp. 32-3 of the "Guide to Royalty Agreements." It should not be necessary for general works.

Clause 17 Some publishers may wish to make special reference in this clause to the National Book Sale, advice on which was given in the Members Circular for March 1963, p. 76, as follows:

> One of two methods of calculating royalties on sales might reasonably be employed:
> 1. The ordinary home rate of royalty (as distinct from the rate of remainders) on the Sale price (i.e. the retail selling price fixed by the publisher for the National Book Sale); or
> 2. The rate of royalty applicable to "cheap editions" (the Sale price being regarded for this purpose as a "cheap edition" price).
> In some cases the royalty might be governed by the special fifty per cent. discount clause which was incorporated in some publishers' contracts.

Clause 18 Publishers generally require not less than *nine* months' notice under this clause. If any advance payment is to be made under the Agreement it is desirable to extend this clause by the words: "provided that the Author shall refund to the Publisher any advance payment as yet unearned made in accordance with Clause [8(a)] hereof." To safeguard against the possibility of reversion while a sub-leased imprint edition is impending, it may also be useful to add: "The Author's requirement that the work be reprinted shall be regarded as satisfied if at the time of the Author's giving notice the Publisher has sub-leased rights for an edition scheduled for publication within twelve months of such notice being given."

Clause 19 No comment required.

Clause 20 This option clause can be adapted to cover the Author's "next work" or "next two works", etc. If it is desired to include an option that is legally enforceable in the strictest sense, the last sentence of the first paragraph of Clause 20 should be amended to read: "Such book or books shall be subject to the same terms as those set out in this Agreement." If the option books are to be on the same terms as the present agreement the new title or titles may be endorsed on that agreement without a new agreement being drawn up. In general however it is more satisfactory to both parties to have a fresh document even though the terms are unchanged. This also has the advantage of further extending the option.

To allow for holiday periods, etc., the Publisher should not generally undertake to exercise his option in less than *two months*.

Appendix 2

AUTHORS' ALTERATIONS
COST MONEY AND CAUSE DELAY

This is the title of a useful leaflet produced by the British Federation of Master Printers in collaboration with the Publishers Association. It is produced on the following pages by special permission. Copies may be bought separately from the Federation; some publishers find its explanations so telling that they buy it in bulk to send out with all proofs going to authors.

Authors' Alterations cost money and cause delay . . .

It is very tempting

to make alterations to proofs.

You can delete a word here . . .

In fact each ~~single~~ alteration
and consequently expensive oper
costs are increased the publishe

change a phrase there . . .

therefore costly work

In fact each single alteration
and ~~consequently expensive oper~~
costs are increased the publishe

put in a comma somewhere else:

In fact each single alteration
and consequently expensive oper
, costs are increased the publishe

there seems nothing to it!

I N FACT, each alteration or addition means laborious and therefore costly work for the printer. If printing costs are increased, the publisher's chance of making the book pay is reduced because he must either raise its price or sell a larger number of copies to cover expenses.

Every single letter and punctuation mark and space in a proof is represented by a tiny piece of metal called 'type'. The printer has had to arrange these in such a way that many pages printed on a large sheet at the same time can be folded so as to come out in the right order. He locks the type in a steel frame to make what he calls a 'forme'. It takes great care and skill to do properly. But it must all be undone again before the smallest alteration can be made. Moreover, every time the forme has to be unlocked there is always the possibility that the pieces of type will slip out of position and cause misprints. Of course the printer knows this and guards against it, but his extra precautions take time and cost money.

The object of this booklet is to demonstrate the cost of making a number of typical alterations. Authors will appreciate that it is to everyone's advantage that they make their alterations while their work is in typescript and not after it is set in printers' type.

Every alteration made in a proof means higher printing costs (which almost certainly will, if the cost of correction exceeds a certain level, be charged to the account of the author). No less important they mean a delay which may result in the postponement of publication date.

Authors' alterations should be kept to the absolute minimum: printers' proofs are intended for checking, not for alteration.

It has been said that authors would dispense with most of their alterations if they had to pay on the spot for making them. There is more than a grain of truth in this.

A high proportion of alterations have to be done by hand—the most expensive way of setting type

Most of the alterations made on proofs are avoidable because they could have been made on the typescript before typesetting began. Too often an author thinks 'Oh! never mind, I can always alter it on the proof.' This attitude is disastrous—it leads straight to extra costs. Even the simplest amendment, so easy to make on a proof, is so time-wasting and costly to carry out. Below are examples of typical alterations to proofs with a brief description of the work they entail and the approximate cost. They are worth a few minutes study.

MAKING CORRECTIONS FROM THE TYPE CASE

Alterations
to single characters

Authors' alterations should be kept to the absolute minimum. Printers' proofs are intended for checking not for alteration.

The author has simply deleted a full point, substituted a colon, altered one letter and inserted a comma. The compositor must lift the 2nd and 3rd lines of type into his stick, make the corrections, respace the lines, and replace them. The type will be reproofed and checked by the printer. These alterations would cost as much as 4s. Too often an author will inscribe just such avoidable alterations on each page of, say, a 256-pp. book. Such action entails an alteration charge of more than £50.

NOTE: *The examples in this booklet are of text matter which has been set in single characters. Matter set in solid lines or 'slugs' is handled differently but also takes time and costs money to correct.*

RESPACING A LINE OF TYPE AFTER CORRECTING

RESETTING ALTERATIONS ON THE KEYBOARD

Addition and deletion

of words

It is essential that authors' alterations be kept to the absolute minimum. Printers' proofs are intended for correction, not alteration.

A few words added or deleted may mean the respacing of a large number of words by the compositor, or resetting the whole paragraph, with all the subsequent operations. Authors should consider whether the alterations are sufficiently important to warrant the cost, which in this example might be 8s.

Addition and deletion
of sentences and paragraphs

IN FACT, each alteration or addition means laborious and therefore costly work for the printer. If printing costs are increased, the publisher's chance of making the book pay is reduced because he must either raise its price or sell a larger number of copies to cover expenses.

Every single letter and punctuation mark and space in a proof is represented by a tiny piece of metal called 'type'. The printer has had to arrange these in such a way that many pages printed on a large sheet at the same time can be folded so as to come out in the right order. He locks the type in a steel frame to make what he calls a 'forme'. It takes great care and skill to do properly. But it must all be undone again before the smallest alteration can be made. Moreover, every time the forme has to be unlocked there is always the possibility that the pieces of type will slip out of position and cause misprints. Of course the printer knows this and guards against it, but his extra precautions take time and cost money.

Insert n.p. ➤ The object of this booklet is to demonstrate the cost of making a number of typical

[*The invention of movable type has been a great factor in the spread of knowledge and ideas. Movable type also makes possible the alteration of type after it is set, but that additional facility can so easily be misused.*

The addition or deletion of sentences and paragraphs may affect a number of pages. The alteration above made on page 3 of a 16-page section would require the readjustment of subsequent pages. This would entail altering two formes and may cost up to 80*s*.

2	15	14	(3)
7	10	11	6

This diagram shows a typical imposition of a 16-page section in two formes. Pages 3 and 4 are in different formes.

COMPOSITOR UNLOCKING TWO 8-PAGE FORMES IN ORDER TO READJUST THE PAGES.

8	9	12	5
1	16	13	(4)

Authors! You can help
to keep costs down

The prevention of authors' alterations is in your hands when you produce the typescript. These three rules will help you to reduce typesetting costs.

1 Type your script

When your typescript is at the printers it will be handled by many people. Hand-written script can be the cause of many queries and mistakes and is much slower to read than typewriting. Type your script on one side of the paper in double spacing—that is the first step in reducing authors' alterations—and number the leaves.

2 Check your typescript

The time to consider alterations is *before* typesetting. Many authors subject their typescripts to two entirely different kinds of checking operations—one to read, re-read, and, if necessary amend until satisfied that the meaning has been conveyed as they wish it to be; a second, to eliminate any inconsistency in style, punctuation, capitalization or spelling. If then the alterations to your typescript are extensive you should have the paragraphs or pages retyped and checked again. It will invariably save time and money.

3 Learn the art of proof-reading

Always use the standard method of proof correction as shown in the following pages. These symbols are clear, unambiguous, and understood by all printers. Their use will become second nature to you in a very short time. Keep your alterations on proofs to the minimum, but where an alteration *is essential*, try to make it in such a way that a minimum amount of extra work is involved. For instance, where it is necessary to add a word, try to delete a word or words of about the same number of letters: if it is necessary to delete a word try to add a word. Similarly, if you add a line, try to knock out a line, even if it is a line of only one word, otherwise the whole paragraph may have to be reset. That is part of the art of sub-editing.

Symbols for correcting proofs

All corrections should be distinct and made in ink in the margins; marks made in the text should be those indicating the place to which the correction refers.

Where several corrections occur in one line, they should be divided between the left and right margins, the order being from left to right in both margins and the individual marks should be separated by a concluding mark.

When an alteration is desired in a character, word, or words, the existing character, word, or words should be struck through and the character to be substituted written in the margin, followed by a concluding stroke (/).

Where it is desired to change one character only to a capital letter, the word 'cap' should be written in the margin. Where, however, it is desired to change more than one character, or a word or words, in a particular line, to capitals, then one marginal reference 'caps' should suffice, with the appropriate symbols made in the text as required.

Normally, only matter actually to be inserted or added to the existing text should be written on the proof. If, however, any comments or instructions are written on the proof, they should be encircled and preceded by the word PRINTER (in capitals and underlined).

MARGINAL MARK	MEANING	CORRESPONDING MARK IN TEXT
/	Correction is concluded	None
New matter followed by /	Insert in text the matter indicated in margin	⋏
ℐ	Delete	Strike through characters to be deleted
ℐ	Delete and close up	Strike through characters to be deleted and use mark
stet	Leave as printed	• • • • under characters to remain
ital.	Change to italic	——— under characters to be altered
s.c.	Change to even small capitals	═══ under characters to be altered
caps	Change to capital letters	≡≡≡ under characters to be altered
c.& s.c.	Use capital letters for initial letters and small capitals for rest of words	——— under initial letters and ═══ under the rest of the words
bold	Change to bold type	∿∿∿ under characters to be altered
l.c.	Change to lower case	Encircle characters to be altered
rom.	Change to roman type	Encircle characters to be altered
w.f.	Wrong fount. Replace by letter of correct fount	Encircle character to be altered

MARGINAL MARK	MEANING	CORRESPONDING MARK IN TEXT
ꝗ	Invert type	Encircle character to be altered
X	Change damaged character(s)	Encircle character(s) to be altered
7 under character (e.g. 𝓍⁷)	Substitute or insert character(s) under which this mark is placed, in 'superior' position	/ through character or ʌ where required
⋀ over character (e.g. 𝓍⋀)	Substitute or insert character(s) over which this mark is placed, in 'inferior' position	/ through character or ʌ where required
underline	Underline word or words	——— under words affected
⌒ enclosing ligature or diphthong required	Use ligature (e.g. ffi) or diphthong (e.g. œ)	⌒ enclosing letters to be altered
write out separate letters followed by /	Substitute separate letters for ligature or diphthong	/ through ligature or diphthong to be altered
⌒	Close up—delete space between characters	⌒ linking characters
#	Insert space*	ʎ
#	Insert space between lines or paragraphs*	> between lines to be spaced
less #	Reduce space between lines*	(connecting lines to be closed up
eq #	Make space appear equal between words	| between words
less #	Reduce space between words*	| between words
letter #	Add space between letters*	⦀⦀⦀ between tops of letters requiring space
trs	Transpose	⌐⌐ between characters or words, numbered when necessary
centre	Place in centre of line	Indicate position with ⌐ ¬
☐	Indent one em	⌐
☐☐	Indent two ems	⌐
⌐	Move matter to right	⌐ at left side of group to be moved

*Amount of space and/or length of re-spaced line may be indicated

MARGINAL MARK	MEANING	CORRESPONDING MARK IN TEXT
⌐	Move matter to left	at right side of group to be moved
move	Move matter to position indicated	[ ] at limits of required position
take over	Take over character(s) or line to next line, column or page	⊏
take back	Take back character(s) or line to previous line, column or page	⊐
raise	Raise lines*	over lines to be moved under lines to be moved
lower	Lower lines*	over lines to be moved under lines to be moved
‖	Correct the vertical alignment	‖
═	Straighten lines	═ through lines to be straightened
⊥	Push down space	Encircle space affected
n.p.	Begin a new paragraph	⌐ before first word of new paragraph
run on	No fresh paragraph here	∽ between paragraphs
spell out	Spell out the abbreviation or figure in full	Encircle words or figures to be altered
out see copy	Insert omitted portion of copy NOTE. The relevant section of the copy should be returned with the proof, the omitted portion being clearly indicated.	⋏
,/	Substitute or insert comma	/ through character or ⋏ where required
;/	Substitute or insert semi-colon	/ through character or ⋏ where required
⊙	Substitute or insert full stop	/ through character or ⋏ where required

*Amount of space and/or length of line may be included.

The symbols are extracted from BS 1219: 1958, Recommendations for Proof Correction and Copy Preparation, by permission of the British Standards Institution, 2 Park Street, London W.1, from whom copies of the complete standard may be obtained.

Index